The Year The Panthers Roared

Edited by
Francis J. Fitzgerald

From the
Sports Pages of the

Pittsburgh
Post-Gazette

Published by

AdCraft

Louisville, Ky.

ACKNOWLEDGEMENTS

Chapters 2, 3, 4, 5, 6, 7, 8, 10, 11, 13, 14-sidebar, and 17 have been previously published in *The Pittsburgh Press*. Copyright © 1976 and 1977 by PG Publishing Co. Reprinted by permission of PG Publishing Co. All rights reserved.

Chapters 12, 14, 15-sidebar and 17-sidebar have been previously published in the *Pittsburgh Post-Gazette*. Copyright © 1976 and 1977 by PG Publishing Co. Reprinted by permission of PG Publishing Co. All rights reserved.

"Pitt Wins PSU's Favorite Trophy" reprinted by permission of The Associated Press.

"Dorsett Wins Heisman Trophy" reprinted by permission of United Press International.

Research assistance: Larry Eldridge, Sam Sciullo Jr., Ron Wolf and the University of Pittsburgh Sports Information Office; Fritz Huysman and Tim Rozgonyi and the *Pittsburgh Post-Gazette* library.

ISBN 1-887761-06-3
ISBN 1-887761-09-8 (leatherbound edition)

Book and cover design: Shayne Bowman
Typefaces: Village, Giza from Font Bureau

PUBLISHED BY:
AdCraft Sports Marketing
Kaden Tower, 10th Floor
6100 Dutchman's Lane
Louisville, KY 40205
(502) 473-1124

Royalties to the Pittsburgh Post-Gazette from the sale of this book will be donated to the Dapper Dan Charities Youth Sports Leagues operated by the Boys and Girls Clubs of Western Pennsylvania.

Pittsburgh Post-Gazette

DAPPER DAN
CHARITIES

The Year The Panthers Roared

20 Years Later, Pitt Is Still It

USUALLY THE SHEER JOY AND UNDISPUTED bragging rights that a national champion football team provides its alumni is more than enough to cement forever the team's place in school history. The 1976 University of Pittsburgh team did more, however, than finish with a perfect 12-0 record and bring to the university its ninth national football title.

The team's achievement was even more than Tony Dorsett winning the Heisman Trophy and Johnny Majors being selected national coach of the year for the second time in his first four years at Pitt.

The 1976 Panthers gave football another chance at Pitt. As Dorsett put it years later, "We saved football at Pitt."

During the nine years prior to Majors' arrival in 1973, the Pitt program was the worst in the school's proud 106-year football history. The Panthers were worse than bad. They often weren't competitive.

Under Dave Hart the bottom fell out as the Panthers won only one game in each of three years (1966-68). Hart was replaced in 1969 by Carl DePasqua, a former Pitt player, but success proved elusive. After posting records of 4-6 and 5-5 in his first two seasons, DePasqua's Panthers fell to 3-8 in 1971 and 1-10 in 1972.

After nine straight losing seasons and eight losses in nine years to arch-rival Penn State, Pitt Chancellor Wesley Posvar decided enough was enough. He made two decisions after the 1972 season that would ensure Pitt's return from the football graveyard.

Posvar's first move was to get Pitt out of the so-called Big-Four Agreement with Penn State, Syracuse and West Virginia. The pact stipulated that member schools would play with fewer scholarships than the NCAA norm and prohibited redshirting.

It was Posvar's belief that the agreement had frozen the competitive advantage in favor of the

JANUARY 10, 1977   ONE DOLLAR

PITT IS IT!

DORSETT 33

appearances in Cyclones history.

One of Majors' initial moves was to get a commitment from Dorsett to play football at Pitt. By getting the 157-pound wisp from Hopewell High School in nearby Aliquippa, Pa., Majors ensured that his first Pitt recruiting class would be memorable.

But, Majors and his chief lieutenant, Jackie Sherrill, didn't stop with Dorsett. They ensured that the first class would be legendary by adding quarterback Robert Haygood, tight end Jim Corbett, placekicker Carson Long, linebackers Arnie Weatherington and Cecil Johnson, defensive linemen Al Romano, Don Parrish and Gary Burley, a junior college transfer, and offensive linemen John Pelusi and John Hanhauser.

The next year Majors struck gold again, getting commitments from quarterback Matt Cavanaugh, running back Elliott Walker, defensive lineman Randy Holloway, defensive back Bob Jury, wide receiver Willie Taylor and offensive guard Tom Broza.

With the addition of wide receiver Gordon Jones and offensive lineman Matt Carroll in 1975, the rebuilding was complete.

Pitt showed immediate improvement, winning six games in 1973, seven in 1974 and eight the next year. The Panthers played in the Fies-

other member schools.

The second move toward football respectability came when Posvar and Athletic Director Cas Myslinski hired Majors as head coach.

A 37-year-old former great tailback at Tennessee, Majors had just put hapless Iowa State on the football map with the first two bowl

---

Pitt's 1976 national championship revived the Panthers' once proud football power.

ta Bowl following the 1973 season, marking Pitt's first bowl appearance in 17 years.

Just as important, the winning rekindled fan interest in Pitt football.

The average attendance at Pitt Stadium rebounded from a 22-year low of 21,000 in 1972 to 42,000 in 1975, then the fifth highest in school history.

The 1975 Panthers ended the season ranked in both wire service polls from the first time since 1963. With 18 of 22 starters returning in 1976, Pitt was expected to be very good but none of the pollsters dared predict what was ahead.

Pitt didn't waste any time showing the nation what had, defeating Notre Dame, 31-10, in a nationally televised season opener at South Bend. The game was highlighted by Dorsett's 181-yard rushing performance.

Touchdown Tony set the tone for the most memorable season in modern Pitt football history on the Panthers' first offensive play against the Irish. Notre Dame had driven the length of the field to take a 7-0 lead when Dorsett exploded for a 61-yard run that set up the tying touchdown.

Dorsett's performance was even more amazing when you consider that Irish coach Dan Devine had installed several new defensive looks in an effort to stop, or at least slow down, Dorsett. As a junior, Dorsett had rushed for 303 yards against Notre Dame at Pitt Stadium.

The first major hurdle of the 1976 season presented itself the next week when Haygood, the starting senior quarterback, went down for the season with a knee injury at Georgia Tech.

No problem. Cavanaugh, a junior, finished the game and proved to be more than an adequate replacement when in Week 4 he completed 14 of 17 passes for 339 yards and five touchdowns in a 44-31 victory at Duke.

But, the injury jinx struck again when Cavanaugh fractured an ankle the next week against Louisville. Majors came up with a replacement in Tom Yewcic, a walk-on who once had ranked ninth on the quarterback depth chart.

The junior from Conemaugh, Pa., filled in capably and held the offense together against Miami, Navy and Syracuse. Cavanaugh returned the next week against Army.

It was during this difficult period that Dorsett took center stage and laid his claim to the Heisman. In his final seven games, Dorsett averaged 215 yards rushing per game en route to leading the nation in rushing with 1,948 yards.

Against Navy in Annapolis Dorsett became the NCAA all-time leading rusher, breaking the record of 5,177 yards set the previous year by Archie Griffin of Ohio State.

When Dorsett broke the record with a 32-yard touchdown run in the fourth quarter, the 4,000-member brigade of Midshipmen gave him a standing ovation of nearly four minutes.

The Panthers moved into the No. 1 spot in both The Associated Press and United Press International polls in the ninth week after Purdue upset previous top-ranked Michigan.

Dorsett's 224 yards rushing and two touchdowns in a 24-7 victory over Penn State at Three Rivers Stadium in Pittsburgh in the final regular season game nailed down Pitt's first win over the Nittany Lions since 1965 and the Panthers' first unbeaten season since 1937.

After the game, Paterno called Dorsett the greatest running back to perform against any of his Penn State teams. When an inquiring reporter asked him to elaborate on Dorsett's skills, Paterno answered, "How many ways can you say great?"

Despite all of the pre-game hype, the national championship game against Georgia in the Sugar Bowl was anti-climactic.

The tough but unheralded Pitt defense completely out-classed Georgia's better known Junkyard Dog defense. The Panthers intercepted four Bulldog passes in the first half and led, 21-0, at the break. Georgia escaped a shutout in the third quarter with a 25-yard field goal that was set up by a Pitt fumble.

Following the game, Georgia coach Vince Dooley added to the praise heaped upon Pitt by opponents almost on a weekly basis throughout the regular season. "The most complete football team I've ever faced," he said of the Panthers.

Years later the accolades were still rolling in. *The Sporting News* in 1987 selected the 1976 Pitt team as the 17th best in college football history. The 50th anniversary issue of the *Street & Smith* college preview magazine in 1990 rated Pitt '76 the 13th best college team since 1940.

But, *Sports Illustrated* perhaps said it best about the team that saved football at Pitt. On the *SI* cover the week after the Sugar Bowl, Cavenaugh and Dorsett are featured in celebration. The photo headline simply reads: "Pitt Is It."

Nearly 20 years later, that *SI* cover picture is still on display at several locations around the Pitt campus.

FRITZ HUYSMAN
Assistant Managing Editor/Sports
Pittsburgh Post-Gazette
June 19, 1996

The Year Pitt Owned the College Football World

By Marino Parascenzo

Johnny Majors doesn't really have a laugh. What he has is something like a cross between a wheeze and a cackle, like when a gasket blows on an old tractor. Whatever it is, on a hot August day in 1973, in Johnstown, Pa., Johnny Majors, in his first year as coach of the Pitt Panthers, had the first laugh.

This was when Tony Dorsett carried the ball for the first time with the Pitt Panthers. Dorsett, the most heralded freshman in the land that year, had arrived at Pitt's Johnstown campus for fall camp listed No. 4 on the tailback depth chart. There was no No. 5.

Are you serious? the press asked.

"He hasn't done anything yet," Majors argued, in a textbook case of flawless logic.

So in the first contact drills, tailbacks Nos. 1, 2 and 3 took their turns hitting the line. Then Dorsett stepped up for his first try. Majors was standing to the side, facing the play, his back to the restless press corps.

Dorsett took the handoff, did a little dance, then burst through the line and was gone, 60-some yards, untouched. It was over quickly. The play was breathtaking.

Without a word, Majors slowly turned his head and looked back over his left shoulder. He wasn't cackling, but he was grinning — like a guy who had just hit a straight flush right in the belly.

It was the summer of 1973. Pitt's 1976 national championship had just been born.

★ ★ ★

The Pitt Panthers were hardly a surprise team when the '76 season arrived. They were already a national force. You had your Tony Dorsett, for example, a nifty defense led by Don Parrish and Al Romano, and Johnny Majors was doing his smashing cornpone act. The Panthers had ended the '75 season with a win in the Sun Bowl, contrary to what one Pitt player suggested, the visit to El Paso was worth more than just a

Pitt's journey to No. 1 in 1976 was capped off with a 27-3 win over Georgia in the Sugar Bowl.

good bottle of tequila for a buck and a half over in Juarez. The win put more real muscle into their growing reputation. But still, as far as the pollsters were concerned, the Panthers were still Eastern football, and Eastern football still was not respected. If the '76 Panthers wanted to win the national championship, first they had to get someone's attention.

This they did by hitting the football world in the head with a 2 x 4 named Notre Dame. That is, they thumped Notre Dame, 31-10, in the '76 season-opener.

So much for the first step. Next came a cosmic chess game. Somewhere, two supernatural guys were sitting at a board, trying to one-up each other by shoving Pitt around.

"I'm going to get Robert Haygood hurt."

"Oh, yeah? Well, then I'll make Matt Cavanaugh a star."

"OK, I'll hurt him, too."

"Yeah? Then I'll send in Tom Yewcic."

"Who?"

"Tom Yewcic."

"Who's he?"

"Just wait."

The chess game also included a friendly schedule made years in advance, and Southern Cal getting beat, and then Purdue, mind you, knocking off Michigan at precisely the decisive moment. Pitt would have a few sweaty moments, then go unbeaten, get voted No. 1, them whomp Georgia in the Sugar Bowl, and

that was it: national championship.

It would be a season of ridiculous ease at some points, some routine public executions, some clutch performances, and a couple of heart-stoppers. Pitt was real, but needed to convince the world. They started with that attention-getter.

Before the game, the Panthers noticed that the grass at Notre Dame Stadium was up over shoe tops. High enough, say, to slow down Tony Dorsett. Majors grinned. "I guess I shouldn't say anything," he said, "because I'm not in charge of mowing."

Dorsett had ruined Notre Dame single-handed with 303 yards rushing in 1975, and the Irish vowed never again. In a way, they were right. He got only 181 yards this time.

The Irish took a 7-0 lead, and the game was over. Dorsett blasted for 61 yards on his first carry, and tied the game on a 5-yard bang. Robert Haygood, the quick option quarterback, darted in for two touchdowns in the second period. In the fourth, in a preview of things to come, Matt Cavanaugh, the No. 2 QB, sliced in from 8 yards out for a TD. And the defense sacked QB Rick Slager five times. Pitt's 31-10 win set off lights all over the country.

Twenty years later, in 1996, Johnny Majors would think back over that team and consider its strongest point.

"That was a team," he said, "that had no weakness."

Georgia Tech was strictly no contest, not even at home in Atlanta. This was a 42-14 exercise. Dorsett gained 113 yards and scored three TD's from 5, 6 and 10 yards, but the key moment came early in the second period. Bobby Haygood was scrambling on an option-keeper, slipped trying to cut, and was hit. Word came quickly from the locker room: torn ligaments, out for the season.

"Haygood's loss is a tremendous blow to our team," Majors would say after the game. "And that's an understatement."

Matt Cavanaugh, a quiet and easy smiling junior out of Youngstown, Ohio, got his turn. Cavanaugh didn't have the darting speed of Haygood, but he had twice the arm. And he was scary cool for a junior. He would be the perfect complement to the electrifying running of Dorsett. He finished up against Georgia Tech, directing the Panthers to five of their six TD's. He scored himself on a 4-yard run, went 7-for-13 passing for 117 yards and one TD.

With the game out of reach, another guy played quarterback for Pitt. He was Tom Yewcic — Tom Who? — a senior from Conemaugh, Pa., near Johnstown. He was the scout team QB. This was his first game action. Majors was down to two serviceable QB's, and he had to give the distant second some real work. He also would reward him for all the practice work. Yewcic would be just another also-played in the small type in the Sunday paper. What really hap-

The Road to No. 1

Date	Opponent	Score
Sept. 11, 1976	Notre Dame	31-10
Sept. 18, 1976	Georgia Tech	42-14
Sept. 25, 1976	Temple	21-7
Oct. 2, 1976	Duke	44-31
Oct. 9, 1976	Louisville	27-6
Oct. 16, 1976	Miami (Fla.)	36-19
Oct. 23, 1976	Navy	45-0
Oct. 30, 1976	Syracuse	23-13
Nov. 6, 1976	Army	37-7
Nov. 13, 1976	West Virginia	24-16
Nov. 26, 1976	Penn State	24-7
Jan. 1, 1977	Georgia	27-3

pened, though, is that the heavy hand of prophecy had just tapped Yewcic and the Pitt Panthers.

A schedule made up years in advance was working out dandy, and it contained a comparatively recent addition, the Temple Owls, from across the state, in Philadelphia. Temple was trying to build its program and loaded up with Pitt and Penn State, but proved to be much more than the anticipated workout. The Panthers' shut-out defense kept things in perspective. Anyone expecting a Tony Dorsett blowout had to settle for 112 yards and a short TD. His running mate, Elliott Walker, who would have been a star alongside a lesser light, also scored. The 21-7 win gave the No. 3 ranked

Panthers a 3-0 record.

The fates had a perverse sense of humor. They set the Panthers up one week, and knocked them down the next. Things were going swimmingly for the Panthers under their new quarterback. They'd got past Temple on unsteady legs, then Cavanaugh really hit his stride against Duke. He went 14-for-17 for 339 yards and a Pitt record five TD's, and what balance — two to flanker Willie Taylor, two to split end Gordon Jones, one to tight end Jim Corbett. It was a 44-31 decision.

No disrespect intended, but Louisville, the next obstacle, was not one of the Godzillas of college football. And if they seemed a soft spot on the Pitt schedule, were they any softer than, say Rice in the Southwest Conference? Or Northwestern in the Big Ten? On a dreary, rainy October day in Pitt Stadium, the Panthers had no real trouble winning, 27-6. But fate struck again, the hard way. Cavanaugh, who had scored twice on runs of 17 and 6 yards, came up limping from an option play. It was a hairline fracture of the left shinbone. The Panthers were 5-0 now, and ranked No. 2 in the nation, and had just lost their second quarterback in three weeks. Cavanaugh would be out three to four weeks. Tom Yewcic came in to stabilize the offense and protect a 27-0 lead, and the defense kept Louisville quiet.

"When Robert got hurt, I was nervous," said Yewcic, the great unknown. "When Matt got hurt, I didn't have time. It's a honor running this team. But it's sort of scary at the same time."

Tom Yewcic got the call. Who was this Tom Yewcic? He was a dream-struck kid, a former ninth-stringer who so loved the game he'd stayed as a walk-on at Pitt just to be part of the team.

"Here's a guy who'd taken his lumps, got beaten around on the scout squad," Majors said. "He was tough, heady, and cool. It was Wednesday before the Miami game that I decided to start him."

The season had reached its second crisis. The Panthers were edgy.

"I don't like to see just anybody come up and play quarterback," said offensive tackle John Hanhauser, "because not just anybody can."

"It don't make any difference to me who gets the ball to me," said Dorsett, "but it will be a different situation to us all with a new quarterback in there."

Not that they had much choice. Pitt obviously was not wallowing in quarterbacks. Yewcic was it. But first Majors would have to retool the offense for him.

"I became concerned about the defense keying on Dorsett, trying to take him out of the game," Majors said. "So I put the 'I' formation back in a little, but we still had the veer, and I put in the pitch and the sprint draw. And I put in some play action to get Yewcic deep in the backfield. He did a wonderful job."

In the summer of 1996, shortly before camp opened for the San Francisco 49ers, Cavanaugh,

their quarterback coach, looked back: "Yeah, I thought, why me? I felt I was in the midst of something good. Then selfishly, you think, they can't do it without me. And then when they don't miss a beat, you say, do they even miss me?"

Yewcic's career consisted of three games. With forgivable hyperbole, his role can be likened to a lifesaver who, all he did, was save three lives.

There was the Miami game, a 36-19 victory.

"Five minutes before the game, when I was warming up, Coach Majors asked me if I was ready to go, and I said I'm as ready as I'll ever be," Yewcic said. "And he said, 'Good — you're starting.'"

Yewcic threw seven passes, hit on two against Miami, including a 40-yard scoring strike to Dorsett. Dorsett had his best game of the season to date, 227 yards on 35 carries. Next was the 45-0 win over Navy at Annapolis. Dorsett rushed for 180 yards, and with a 32-yard touch-

Johnny Majors' braintrust: The 1976 Panther coaching staff.

down run in the fourth quarter set the NCAA major college career rushing record with 5,206 yards. Yewcic had the distinction of handing off to him on that carry.

Next came a real scare. Syracuse had come to Pitt Stadium bearing an unknown sophomore quarterback named Bill Hurley. The Panthers, ranked No. 4 in the country in defense, couldn't handle the guy. Hurley threw for 303 yards, and the game was still much in doubt late in the fourth quarter. Pitt's defense finally removed all doubt. Pitt was hanging on to a 20-13 lead, and Syracuse was hammering at the door, sitting on third-and-1 at the Pitt 11. Fullback John Sessler slammed into the line, and was stopped inches short of the first down. Then, he got the call again. Pitt tackle Don Parrish stood him up, and linebacker Arnie Weatherington hit him higher. Sessler could not so much as lean for those last precious inches. Pitt took over, Dorsett ripped off runs of 28 and 33 yards, and Carson Long kicked a 22-yard field goal to lock up the game, a 23-13 victory. Pitt was now 8-0, but still not No. 1.

But the crisis had passed.

"Tom did what he was supposed to do in practice with the scout team, and took a beating," Cavanaugh was saying, these 20 years later. "The players understood. And when he came in, he plugged right into an offense that was rolling. I will never forget what he did. He did more than was expected of him."

The Panthers were coming down the stretch now, Cavanaugh was back, and Army was next, the first week of November. The Panthers would make some history this week. The No. 1-ranked team in the football polls, like a boxing champion, rarely can be defrocked without getting knocked out. Pitt would bounce Army, 37-7, and late in the game the fans at Pitt Stadium erupted. Word came over the public address system that Purdue had knocked off No. 1 Michigan. The Panthers were whooping it up, but were workmanlike. Dorsett rushed for 212 yards and three TD's. Cavanaugh hit on 8 of 12 passes for 67 yards and ran for 76 more, and Willie Taylor took a pass for a 24-yard TD play. The Panthers were 9-0 that afternoon.

Majors assembled his team in a meeting Monday morning. "We'll start off with some news you may be interested in," he said. The polls had come out. For the first time since 1937, Pitt was ranked No. 1 in the country.

West Virginia was next, and in a kind of tribute in advance, Dorsett's number, 33, was retired at halftime. He said thanks with 199 yards, and Cavanaugh rushed for 124 of his own. The Mountaineers scored with three minutes left to leave Pitt with a 24-16 win and a 10-0 record. This was the Panthers' final home game of the season. In Pitt Stadium, that is. Penn State was next, but that would be in Pittsburgh's Three Rivers Stadium.

The Pitt-Penn State rivalry had never been of the intensity of say, Texas-Oklahoma or

Alabama-Auburn. This was because Pitt, through de-emphasis, had been so far behind Penn State for so long. Still, it was a pretty good rivalry. Plenty of hype and smoke-blowing. And it was a 7-7 standoff by halftime of that chilly, rainy November night. Then Majors did an interesting thing.

In the second half, Penn State found themselves facing an unbalanced line with Tony Dorsett as the up-back, or fullback in the 'I' formation, and that's generally a blocking back. Where did that come from? The unbalanced line not only thwarted Penn State's defensive schemes, but moving Dorsett to up-back got him a few steps even closer to the line. Penn State was taken completely by surprise.

"That Dorsett is some kind of back," Penn State coach Joe Paterno said. "I didn't think we'd see him at fullback tonight."

Dorsett scored twice, gained 224 yards, and cracked the 6,000-yard rushing mark. Pitt wrapped up a perfect 11-0 regular season, 24-7.

In the bowl hype after the season, an interesting and illogical episode of attempted marketing failed. Michigan coach Bo Schembechler and Southern Cal coach John Robinson both proclaimed that the winner of their Rose Bowl meeting would be the national champion. This despite the fact that both teams had one loss. The nation wasn't buying. The national championship was Pitt's to lose, and Pitt was playing Georgia in the Sugar Bowl.

Pitt headed south earlier than most teams would, to get out of a fierce winter and get some practice time in. The Panthers went to Biloxi, Miss., and it was there that they were all but fitting themselves for championship rings.

Cavanaugh said a feeling had run through the guys when they got South.

"You could just tell, especially at Biloxi," Cavanaugh said. "When we got there, we knew by the way Coach Majors was treating us that he was relaxed. He wasn't uptight.

"His approach showed up," Cavanaugh said, "that this was going to be a breeze."

First, Pitt had to endure a baffling scandal. It developed that the Georgia players had a curfew in New Orleans, but the Pitt players did not. No curfew?

New Orleans sportswriter: "What will their mommies and daddies say?"

Pittsburgh sportswriter: "Mommies and daddies?"

Majors, surprised by the non-issue, made haste to explain that his team was being treated the same on this trip as they were at home. We're an urban school, he said, and we don't have athletic dorms and don't want them, and these guys have to learn to live in this world. The thing was overshadowing the game. Majors imposed a curfew a few nights before the game. It was 2 a.m.

The game strategy was elemental. Majors had put it simply: this was a team without a weakness.

"They've got eight people up there to stop

Tony," Cavanaugh said, "and that means single coverage on our receivers. All you have to do is get them the ball."

Georgia even saw some new stuff. For example, Pitt didn't move on the first series. On the second series, Pitt was second-and-7 at the Georgia 46. Cavanaugh hit fullback Elliott Walker downfield for 36 yards. Before that, Cavanaugh was throwing to the backs only in the flats.

Cavanaugh scored from 6 yards out on that series, hit Gordon Jones with a 59-yarder for another TD, and Dorsett sprinted 11 for another for a 21-0 halftime lead. Carson Long added two field goals in the second half, and the Panthers had a 27-3 victory, a 12-0 record, and the national championship.

Even in victory the party story would not die. The Panthers played the absurdity to the hilt. Defensive lineman Don Parrish, limping in the locker room on a sore ankle, "Oh, it'll be all right, soon as I have a couple of drinks."

Tight end Jim Corbett, "There were times when we had to be in the hotel by 2 a.m. We were in, but sometimes we were in the pool."

(Swimming at 2 a.m.?)

"It was a heated pool."

A New Orleans TV sportscaster on the 10 o'clock news: "The Georgia players are now in bed, and Pitt is just getting dressed to go out."

Another TV news guy: "Majors has posted a curfew. He told them to be in by February."

One cloud hung over this magical time. As the season drew on, rumors became stronger and stronger that Johnny Majors would return to Tennessee as the coach there. Things got feverish just before the Penn State game, when Tennessee coach Bill Battle resigned. The door was open. Was Majors going home? He declined to say.

It didn't help that he was visiting Tennessee in mid-November. He would take the job, of course, but there might have been one moment that gave him pause.

One morning on his visit to Tennessee, he ordered grits for breakfast. The waitress suggested hash-browns. They had no grits.

Maybe the entire season was wrapped up in one vignette just before the Sugar Bowl game, when Tony Dorsett was introduced to Georgia safety Chuck Mitchell.

"This is the last man who has a chance to stop you," Dorsett was told.

"If we should meet, say, at the 1-yard line," Dorsett said to Mitchell, "why don't you hop on my back? That'll make it easier for both of us."

Not that Dorsett carried this no-weakness Pitt team. Far from it. But it was that kind of talent and confidence and attitude that pretty much captured the 1976 championship season.

The charm of Pitt's magical season of 1976 captured the entire city of Pittsburgh.

Tony & Pitt's 'D' Crush Irish, 31-10

20

By Russ Franke
Special to The Pittsburgh Press

South Bend, Ind. — It was a bad day for the Irish and a great day for Pitt and Tony Dorsett, but the fleet Panther running back thought yesterday was an even greater day for the Pitt defense.

After he had punished Notre Dame again as only he can do, Dorsett stepped aside and gave all the credit for the Panthers' impressive 31-10 win to the defensive team.

"Our defense won it for us," he said, even though a coast-to-coast television audience and a capacity crowd of 59,035 had eyes only for the flying young man who is well on his way to becoming collegiate football's all-time leading rusher.

Dorsett ripped off 181 yards against a defense that had vowed to come up with something to stop him following his 303-yard performance in last year's meeting.

In a much-ballyhooed game that was supposed to be an even battle for early recognition as a national championship contender, the slightly favored Irish set the Panthers back on their heels by driving 86 yards for the first score, featured by the running of Jerome Heavens and Al Hunter.

But Dorsett turned the game around the first time he carried the ball. He burned the Irish with a 61-yard bolt that set up the tying touchdown, and the Pitt secondary picked off a pair of passes by ND quarterback Rick Slager to set up two more touchdowns, on plunges by Robert Haygood early in the second period.

Thus the ninth-ranked Panthers got themselves off to a rousing start in 1976 and will be favored to win their next nine games, starting at Georgia Tech next Saturday night.

Notre Dame had a 20-12 edge in first downs, but was outplayed, and it sounds much like the way the Panthers used to lose ball games before the Johnny Majors era.

Notre Dame scored on its first possession with a strong ground attack that carried to the Pitt 25, Jerome Heavens and Hunter getting most of the yardage with some good deception

Pitt took control of the game after Tony Dorsett's 61-yard run.

by Slager on the handoffs.

With the ball on the 25, Slager flipped a pass into the left flat to Ken McAfee and the all-America tight end galloped into the end zone untouched. Dave Reeve's kick made it 7-0.

Then it was Pitt's turn. It took the Panthers less than two minutes to get even. On his first carry, Dorsett drew a gasp from the fired-up crowd when he weaved his way 61 yards behind great downfield blocking to the Irish 23. Clipping set the ball back to the 31 but, after Haygood picked up 6 yards, he passed 19 yards to Jim Corbett at the 6.

Dorsett skipped around right end from there for the score and Carson Long's kick tied it.

Tight defense by both teams turned the rest of the first period into a punting duel between Larry Swider and ND's Joe Restic, Notre Dame meanwhile losing defensive tackle Jeff Weston with a knee injury.

And then Pitt got the first break of the day early in the second period.

With the ball on the Irish 22, Slager threw a pass right into the hands of the Panthers' Leroy Felder, all alone at the 37, and Felder raced to the 2. After Bobby Hutton got a yard, Haygood dove over the top for a touchdown. Long made it 14-7.

Disaster struck the Irish again less than a

minute later when Jeff Delaney, the monster linebacker, picked off a Slager pass intended for McAfee over the middle at the ND 33.

The Pitt offensive line went to work again, opening enough daylight for Dorsett to rip off gains of 7 and 14 yards to the 1. Once again, Haygood went over the top for the score. Long converted for a 21-7 lead.

The Panthers gave the Irish a chance when

Dorsett's 181 yards and 2 TD's proved to be too much for the Irish.

Gordon Jones dropped Restic's punt and ND recovered on the Pitt 23. But Cecil Johnson sacked Slager on the 36, and when Reeve tried a 44-yard field goal it was wide left.

But a nice punt return by Randy Harrison to the Pitt 45, and runs of 8 and 7 yards by Heavens and 7 by Hunter moved the Irish into scoring position again. The Panthers appeared to be out of danger when Al Romano sacked Slager for a 16-yard loss at the 36, but Reeve brought down the house by booting a 53-yard field goal to cut the lead to 21-10. It was a Notre Dame record, erasing a 49-yarder by Joe Perkowski in 1961.

Pitt had an opportunity with time running out in the half when Haygood hit Corbett with passes of 17 and 23 yards to the ND 14. Dorsett took a pitchout 8 yards but fumbled into the end zone for a touchback.

Notre Dame began the second half with a brisk march to the Pitt 37, but the drive was turned around when Hunter fumbled and Arnie Weatherington recovered for Pitt on the Panther 44.

Pitt was unable to get anywhere because of the furious rush put on Haygood. However, Swider put Notre Dame in the hole with a 47-yard punt to the 5.

Near the end of the third period, ND was penalized to the Pitt 35 for piling on after a punt, and Cavanaugh came in to quarterback the Panthers.

The Irish had held Pitt to minus yards rushing in the third period, thanks to the pressure put on the quarterback by Willie Fry, Ross Browner and Bob Golic, but the Panther running attack got back into forward gear as the fourth period began.

The Panthers started from the Irish 40 and Cavanaugh picked up 13 yards through the middle after fading to pass, and Dorsett got 10 and 9 yards. The yardage became tougher, however, and after a pitchback to Dorsett went astray for a 12-yard loss, Long kicked a perfect 34-yard field goal for a 24-10 lead.

Restic, ordinarily a reliable punter, had the misfortune of popping one up that went 10 yards to the ND 36. It was the cue Dorsett needed for another brilliant run that silenced the Irish fans.

Dorsett slid to the right, somehow squirmed out of a head-on tackle and got away for 28 yards to the 8, giving him 175 yards for the day and a staggering 748 total for his four games against Notre Dame. Cavanaugh then cut nicely inside tackle and went into the end zone for a touchdown. Long's kick upped the score to 31-10.

SCORE BY PERIODS

Pitt	7	14	0	10	–	31
Notre Dame	7	3	0	0		10

23

Pitt Wrecks Georgia Tech, 42-14

24

BY RUSS FRANKE
Special to The Pittsburgh Press

Atlanta — Pitt enhanced its early image as a national power by obliterating Georgia Tech, 42-14, last night before a crowd of 43,424 at Grant Field.

The Panthers combined the running talent of Tony Dorsett (113 yards rushing and three touchdowns) with the passing of Robert Haygood and Matt Cavanaugh, plus another solid defensive effort to prove that their 31-10 win over Notre Dame last week was legitimate.

However, the Panthers lost the services of Haygood for perhaps the remainder of the season when Haygood suffered torn ligaments of the left knee in the second period.

Prior to this, Haygood bit a huge chunk of Tech territory by slashing off right tackle 36 yards to the Yellow Jacket 10 just past the middle of the first quarter.

Until then it was all defense and punting with Pitt's Larry Swider getting off a 60-yarder to the 17 and a 77-yarder to the 10.

Meanwhile, Randy Holloway, Jim Cramer and Don Parrish led the Pitt defense in preventing the Jackets from threatening in the first quarter. Parrish got one sack and recovered a fumble at midfield by David Sims, a tailback playing his first game at fullback.

Georgia Tech also knocked loose a fumble when Haygood was hit cocking his arm for a pass and Bob Kupper recovered the ball.

Once again the Panther front wall rocked the ball loose early in the second quarter just after Tech substituted freshman Mike Jolly for Bucky Shamburger. Eddie Lee Ivory fumbled the handoff and Ed Wilamowski recovered at the Tech 39.

The Panthers parlayed this break into another Dorsett touchdown after seven plays with Cavanaugh at quarterback. Walker picked up 5 yards, Dorsett 9 and Cavanaugh 6.

With the ball on the 5 after two more plays, Dorsett took a pitchout around right end for a 5-yard touchdown. Long made it 14-0.

The Yellow Jackets came right back with a 71-yard kickoff return to the Pitt 28 by Drew

---

Dorsett's sparkling performance of 113 yards and 3 TD's ensured a Pitt victory.

Hill, but the Pitt defense held and Danny Smith's 39-yard field goal attempt was wide left.

Dorsett got his team out of the hole with a 19-yard dash through the middle but Tech tightened up and Swider punted 46 yards to the Tech 15.

Toward the end of the first half, the Yellow Jackets turned their wishbone into a razzle-dazzle offense and it paid off.

On a reverse pitchout, Hill rambled 16 yards to the Pitt 33. The next play was even fancier and it was good for 31 yards to the 2 when Rucker went wide with a pitchout and threw a halfback pass to the other halfback, Ivory.

A roughing penalty put the ball on the 1 and Jolly dived over the top for a touchdown. Smith kicked the point that cut the lead to 14-7.

The scoring drive came just when it appeared Pitt would be in position to score again. With Tech's Harper Brown back to punt,

Majors (left) and his two quarterbacks, Robert Haygood (10) and Matt Cavanaugh (12).

the snap was high and the ball was downed on the Jacket 23, but a flag was thrown against Pitt for a personal foul and Tech kept the ball.

A holding penalty and some more aggressive defense enable Pitt to run the lead up to 21-7 before three minutes had gone by in the second half.

The penalty moved the ball back to the 18 and on the next play, defensive backs Jeff Delaney and J.C. Wilson penetrated and Wilson tipped a pitchout toward the goal line and Holloway recovered the fumble on the Tech 4. After Dorsett was stopped for no gain, Cavanaugh rolled left and easily went in for the score. Long added the extra point.

The Yellow Jackets got that touchdown back in a hurry after Walker fumbled and Reggie Wilkes recovered for Tech on the Panther 37.

On the next play, Jolly passed 36 yards to split end John Steeler behind the secondary to the 1. Jolly plunged over right tackle for the score and Smith's conversion made it 24-14.

Then it was the Panthers' turn to retaliate quickly — in six plays. After Dorsett ran for 7 and Cavanaugh picked up a first down, Tech was penalized 15 yards to the Pitt 49 for a late hit.

Gordon Jones dropped a first-down pass but compensated sensationally on the next play when he beat the secondary and took Cavanaugh's pass up the middle for 51 yards for a touchdown.

The accent switched to offense, and Pitt began a march from its 28 into Tech territory as Cavanaugh hit Willie Taylor for 12 yards and Dorsett made some moderate gains that put him over 100 yards rushing for the game at the end of the third period.

The Panthers got into short range when Cavanaugh hit Jones with a 26-yard pass to the 7. Dorsett was nailed for a 3-yard loss but on the next play he flashed his explosive style by darting 10 yards untouched through the left side and the Panthers had a 35-14 lead on Long's conversion.

It became a complete runaway in the middle of the final period when Jolly's pass went off the fingertips of Elliott Price and Leroy Felder intercepted and returned 10 yards to the Tech 33. The Jackets hit Felder out of bounds for a personal foul and the penalty put the ball on the 18.

Cavanaugh got a first down at the 6 with a 2-yard dive and Walker carried to the 6, where Cavanaugh found Jones with a pass in the end zone. Long upped the score to 42-14.

SCORE BY PERIODS

Pitt	7	7	14	14	–	42
Georgia Tech	0	7	7	0	–	14

Pitt Survives Temple Scare, 21-7

By Russ Franke
Special to The Pittsburgh Press

Pittsburgh — It was supposed to be a good day for Pitt to impress the poll-takers, but the Panthers didn't even impress themselves in yesterday's home opener at Pitt Stadium.

Kept off balance by an unconventional Temple team, Pitt managed to escape the wave of upsets that have been engulfing the nation's powers, and managed to come from behind to win, 21-7, thanks mostly to its defense. And as a relieved Johnny Majors said afterward, "It's the mark of a good team to win even on its bad days."

Temple blocked a punt and turned it into a touchdown in the first period and came up with some things Majors credited as "clever," but they only served to delay the inevitable as Tony Dorsett's running and Jim Corbett's pass catching finally allowed the Panther offense to catch up with the defense.

"It's hard to go out week in and week out and be mentally high unless you're playing Notre Dame or Southern Cal every week," said Dorsett, who survived another pounding and for a time appeared to be finished for the day.

He went down with a bruised calf in the first period but still came back and gained 112 yards on 23 carries, his 10th straight 100-plus game, to move that much closer to the all-time collegiate career rushing championship.

He needs 638 yards in the remaining eight games to surpass Ohio State's Archie Griffin, or just under 80 yards a game.

A crowd of 38,500 waited patiently for the Panthers to begin looking like the nation's No. 3-ranked team and Temple, unimpressed by the Pitt image, tried the Panthers' patience sorely.

A lot of the credit for Temple's tough showing had to go to Owls coach Wayne Hardin, whose sleeper play caused a great deal of unpleasant commotion and helped beat Pitt in 1962 when he was the Navy coach.

His tactic yesterday was an ingenious and original ruse on Temple punts that caught the Panthers off-guard twice. Temple would give the appearance of running the ball on fourth

Jim Corbett (81) snags a pass from Matt Cavanaugh for eight yards.

down and suddenly rush in the punter while Pitt was trying to get its specialty teams on the field.

The first time it forced Pitt to call a time out, and the second time it cost Pitt 15 yards for having too many men (about 16) involved on the play.

Hardin said he got the idea from watching last year's film and spent 15 minutes on it during the week because "Pitt has a great punt return team."

Pitt blew a chance to score on its first series and on its next possession fell behind by seven points. Matt Cavanaugh, quarterbacking the entire game, passed 34 yards to flanker Willie Taylor to get Pitt into field position on the Temple 35, and Dorsett rambled for gains of 6 and 14 yards. When the drive stalled, Carson Long tried a 30-yard field goal that was wide.

With five minutes left in the first period, Temple put the rush on punter Larry Swider at the Pitt 30 and Bruce Gordon blocked the kick. Chuck Giff, who played midget football with Dorsett in Aliquippa, scooped up the ball and

Al Romano (91) and Randy Holloway (70) wrap up Temple quarterback Pat Carey.

ran 15 yards for a touchdown. Wes Sornisky kicked the extra point.

Pitt got another opportunity when Anthony Anderson fumbled Pat Carey's pitchout and Bob Jury recovered for Pitt on the Owl 18. Dorsett ripped off 11 yards and on the next play into the line had to leave with an injury. Elliott Walker lost the ball in a pileup on the following play and Rich Dowiak got the ball for Temple.

The Panther defense, once again asserting itself, forced a punt that fell short and after three plays, Long came through with a perfect 50-yard field goal and the lead was cut to 7-3.

Long trimmed it to 7-6 after the Panthers put a good rush on Carey and knocked loose a fumble on the Owl 38. Ed Wilamowski recovering for Pitt. After Dorsett slashed through for gains of 7 and 13 yards and left the game limping again, Long sent through a 33-yard field goal.

The Panthers finally got ahead when they came out of the dressing room after what had to be a "refreshing" halftime talk by Majors. Finally clicking after an erratic first half, the Panther offense shoved the ball down Temple's throat.

The pain in his leg eased by ice packs on the sideline, Dorsett ran as if 100 percent healthy on the first series and he had plenty of help from fullback Elliott Walker. They gained 60 yards between them on an 82-yard drive that was helped along by Cavanaugh's 11-yard pass to Jim Corbett, who looked like the best tight end in the country.

Walker got the touchdown on a 1-yard dive and Dorsett skipped around the left end with a pitchout for a two-point conversion that made it 14-7.

Casey Murphy, whose pinpoint punting helped the Temple cause more than once, kicked the ball to the 2-yard line and when Pitt was unable to run the ball out of the hole, Larry Swider showed the fans what a real punt looked like.

Swider, who had exploded punts of 60 and 77 yards at Georgia Tech, boomed a 64-yarder to the Temple 32 and after that, the Temple team was done for the day offensively.

The Pitt front five of Al Romano, Don Parrish, Randy Holloway, Cecil Johnson and Ed Wilamowski did their disruptive best in keeping Temple bottled up, and the Panthers scored their insurance touchdown early in the fourth period.

Johnson and Leroy Felder teamed up to bat a Carey pass into the air and Jury made an interception while falling at the Pitt 35.

The Panthers marched the ball in on 10 plays. Bobby Hutton's 11-yard run and Cavanaugh's 20-yard pass to Corbett were the big plays in addition to a personal foul penalty against Temple, and with the ball on the 3, Dorsett dodged through the left side for the score.

"Technically," said Romano, "we shut them

out but we're still not pleased with our overall play. This was a different type of offense today — they sit back on you and when the ball is snapped it's like who's gonna hit who? They're well-coached and they sort of surprised us."

John Pelusi, the Pitt center, said the Temple defense also played a waiting game and that "it was one of my worst days." He was playing head-to-head against 252-pound Joe Klecko, an all-American candidate who had an outstanding game with eight solo tackles, high on either side.

"Klecko played well," said Pelusi, "but the best nose guard I've ever faced is still Al Romano."

The Panthers, 3-0, play at Duke next Saturday and a letdown there will result in more than the type of minor scare they underwent yesterday.

"With all the upsets going around in college football," said Majors, "I'm just glad to have a win."

SCORE BY PERIODS

Temple	7	0	0	0	–	7
Pitt	0	6	8	7	–	21

Temple's quarterback attempts to avoid being sacked by Pitt linebacker Mike Lenosky.

Cavanaugh Powers Panthers, 44-31

34

By Russ Franke
Special to The Pittsburgh Press

Durham, N.C. — The kind of explosive offensive game Pitt was looking for all during the young season showed up yesterday, and although it came from an unexpected quarterback, it was more than enough to whip Duke, 44-31, and keep the Panther record perfect at 4-0.

The explosion didn't come from the Tony Dorsett-Elliot Walker powder keg. It came from the arm of Matt Cavanaugh and some clever routes run by his receivers, Jim Corbett, Gordon Jones and Willie Taylor.

Cavanaugh broke the Pitt record by passing for five touchdowns, breaking the previous high of four by John Hogan and Ivan Toncic, as Pitt took a 44-15 lead before the Blue Devils made a late surge against a tiring defense to prevent it from looking like a runaway.

A drizzle that began at noon eased up shortly after the game started and it held down the crowd to an estimated 37,200 as well as holding down Dorsett for a time on the slick grass.

In the third period, Dorsett topped 100 yards rushing for the 12th straight time, finishing with 129 yards on 31 carries.

The Duke defense also had something to do with it, but the Pitt defense was even better, as usual, especially in the first half when it forced the Blue Devils' slick play-action quarterback, Mike Dunn, to go to the air. Pitt intercepted three of his passes in the first half.

Cavanaugh, getting excellent protection, went 14-for-17 passing, good for 339 yards.

"This is one of the great football games I've been involved in," said Pitt coach Johnny Majors. "With people trying to shut off our option game (and Dorsett) this year, we put in a new passing series last Monday to take advantage of over-aggressive secondaries.

"Dorsett was as valuable to us today as if he would have gained 200 yards."

Dorsett, sore of leg from last week's calf injury plus another vicious pounding, said of the fake-option passing, "This should open things up and open the eyes of our future opponents." The next opponent will be

Matt Cavanaugh had a career day against Duke. His 5 TD passes set a Pitt record.

Louisville next Saturday at Pitt Stadium.

Mike McGee, the Duke coach, said, "We may have made a mistake by putting the emphasis on stopping the run, but Pitt cashed in on our mistakes, which is the sign of a great football team."

In addition to his TD passing mark, Cavanaugh also set a Pitt record with 370 yards total offense, erasing the 331 by Bob Bestwick in 1951 against Michigan State.

Duke took the ball in for a touchdown on its first possession, marching the kickoff 75 yards with the key gains coming on Dunn's passing. The first pass was a 10-yarder to the tight end, Glen Sandefur. After Duke found it difficult to penetrate the middle, Dunn hit split end Tom Hall with a 20-yarder and fullback Tony Benjamin with another 20-yard pass to the Pitt 5.

Two plays later, Art Gore went four yards over the left side with a pitchback for the score. Vince Fusco kicked the extra point.

Pitt went into a hole on Bob Grupp's punt that was downed on the 2. The Panthers got out of trouble temporarily when Cavanaugh threw to tight end Jim Corbett deep in the middle for 41 yards, but they gave the ball right back on Elliott Walker's fumble at midfield. The Blue Devils had to punt, however, when Randy Holloway sacked Dunn on the Pitt 47.

It took the big play for the Panthers to even the score just before the end of the first period. After Cavanaugh had run 6 yards for a first down on the Pitt 34, he passed down the middle to Taylor, the flanker who fought Grupp for the ball and went 66 yards. Carson Long's kick tied it at 7-7.

The Pitt defense began to catch up to the Blue Devils early in the second period. Duke hurt itself with a holding penalty that put the ball back on its 35 and then Al Romano and Cecil Johnson combined to sack Dunn on the 25. When Grupp dropped back to punt, J.C. Wilson blocked it and the ball rocketed through the end zone for a safety that gave Pitt a 9-7 lead.

Pitt moved into Duke territory after a short kickoff and showed a lot of confidence in its defense by going for the sticks on fourth-and-3 on the Duke 33. However, Dorsett was stopped cold and Duke took over. The defense did hold, and Duke was forced to punt.

Near the middle of the period Larry Swider got off a 50-yard punt to the Duke 37, and then the Panthers got their first break. Monster man Jeff Delaney picked off Dunn's quick pass over the middle and returned 7 yards to the 35. Dorsett got some hard yardage, 17 yards in four carries, and with the ball on the 10, Duke end Andy Schoenhoft apparently had Cavanaugh nailed in the backfield.

Cavanaugh, however, kept his feet long enough to fire a pass into the end zone and Taylor made a diving catch for a score. Long converted and it was 16-7.

The Panther defense continued to give Dunn all sorts of problems, Holloway and Dan Parrish nailing the Duke quarterback, and when Grupp punted to the Duke 49, it took Pitt only 41 seconds and four plays to score again.

The Panthers moved into position for the next score on Cavanaugh's 14-yard pass to Taylor on the 31. Cavanaugh picked up four yards on a keeper to the 27 and then found Corbett drifting across the goal line with an easy touchdown pass.

That four-play drive consumed 41 seconds, and the Panthers topped that by striking for another score within seven seconds after Bob Jury intercepted reserve quarterback Dale Oostdyk's pass at midfield and returned it to the Duke 37.

Cavanaugh threw deep down the left side-

Pitt's Willie Taylor (29) hauls in a touchdown pass in the second quarter.

line to Jones at the goal line for the TD and Long's kick made it 30-7.

With the final seconds ticking away, Dunn returned just in time to be intercepted, by Delaney, but time ran out on the Panthers.

It took Pitt 42 seconds into the second half to strike again and give Cavanaugh the touchdown pass record. Dorsett, who was held to 45 yards on 14 carries, got 16 yards on three tries and Walker picked up 12 on a shot through center.

From the Duke 24, Cavanaugh found Jones with a quick throw up the middle at the goal. Long converted for a 37-7 lead.

Duke got on the board in the third quarter but required seven minutes to do it on a 58-yard drive. The score was set up by Mike Barney's 20-yard sweep to the 1. Barney dived over and Dunn passed for two points to Benjamin, cutting the lead to 37-15.

The Panthers got that one back on the next series as Dorsett ripped off 32 yards with a pitchout to the Duke 39, and after Cavanaugh passed 31 yards to Corbett on the 7 and Cavanaugh ran to the 4, Dorsett swept the right side, breaking two tackles, and went in for Pitt's sixth TD.

39

SCORE BY PERIODS

Pitt	7	23	14	0	–	44
Duke	7	0	16	8	–	31

Clever routes by receivers like Gordon Jones (left and above) helped Pitt defeat Duke.

Pitt Wins, 27-6, Loses Cavanaugh

BY RUSS FRANKE
Special to The Pittsburgh Press

Pittsburgh — It was a good news-bad news situation yesterday when Pitt struggled with Louisville in the rain at Pitt Stadium.

The good news was that the Panthers did nothing to hurt their image as the nation's second-ranked team by disposing of the undermanned Cardinals, 27-6, to run their record to 5-0, the best start since 1938.

The bad news was that they lost another quarterback. They had lost Robert Haygood for the season in the second game when his knee was injured badly enough to require an operation. Yesterday they lost Matt Cavanaugh with an ankle injury that will keep him out for at least three weeks as estimated by Dr. James McMaster, the team physician. Cavanaugh went down in the second quarter with what x-rays showed to be a hairline fracture of the left fibula (top of the ankle).

By that time Pitt had piled up a 27-0 lead, and the inexperienced backup men, Tom Yewcic and Dave Migliore, both seniors, were unable to move the offense. Majors attributed it to their lack of previous varsity action, the wet field and poor field positions.

When Majors was asked if he would have a crash program for his surviving quarterbacks this week in getting ready for the toughest opponent on the home schedule, Miami, he said with a weak smile, "I wouldn't use the word crash — let's just say it will be an accelerated program.

"Neither Yewcic nor Migliore had ever played in any kind of a pressure situation before, and both had trouble with the center exchanges. Our regular center couldn't play (John Pelusi, with a knee injury) and the quarterbacks had trouble with the center exchanges.

"In the second half, I was hoping that clock would run like hell, maybe bust a screw loose and go double-time."

The Panther offense looked sharp before Cavanaugh's injury, and Cavanaugh scored the first two touchdowns himself, while Tony Dorsett got off to his 13th straight game as a 100-

Matt Cavanaugh's second-quarter injury against Louisville was a major blow to Pitt.

yards-plus rusher and became the second leading ground-gainer in NCAA history.

The Pitt defense looked sharp all day, rising to the occasion when the offense bogged down, and did not give up a touchdown. Louisville scored on a blocked punt.

Louisville, now 2-2, managed only two first downs rushing and the two alternating quarterbacks, Stu Stram and Roy Steger, were under a severe pass rush throughout by Cecil Johnson, Ed Wilamowski, Al Romano, Don Parrish and Randy Holloway.

The rush was so severe on one play that it resulted in a touchdown when Parrish spun Stram around, Wilamowski knocked the ball loose and Johnson dived on the ball in the end zone for a touchdown. It was the first touchdown ever for Johnson, including his high school days in Miami, Fla.

Pitt drove 54 yards in eight plays for its first score less than five minutes after the kickoff. Dorsett, spelled briefly by Bobby Hutton due to his injured leg, carried five times for 29 yards, including pops of 10 and 11 yards through the middle. The wet turf forced Pitt to limit its outside game, just as the rain limited the crowd to an estimated 20,000 despite the sale of 34,000 tickets.

Cavanaugh passed 15 yards to tight end Jim Corbett, and with the ball on the 17, Cavanaugh showed his vast improvement as a runner by weaving through the pack for a score.

The Panthers made it 10-0 shortly afterward when Leroy Felder recovered Kevin Miller's fumble on the Louisville 18.

Carson Long kicked a 39-yard field goal, his fourth of the year.

Louisville was having a tough enough time with the Pitt defense as it was, but was further damaged by a 56-yard punt by Larry Swider, the No. 2 punter in this nation. Louisville's Dick Pennella punted back to the Pitt 48, and the Panthers drove in for another score early in the second quarter.

Aided by Dorsett's key block, Cavanaugh set up the score with a 21-yard run to the 10 after he had run 13 yards. He scored on a 6-yard effort through the right side and Long's kick made it 17-0.

It went up to 24-0 when Johnson recovered Stram's fumble over the goal, after two plays had been stopped for losses. One of them came when Johnson nailed Calvin Prince, the leading scorer in the country who yesterday was held to 23 yards on 11 carries.

Two minutes later Prince ran into a wall and fumbled, and Pitt monster man Jeff Delaney recovered on the Louisville 31. Dorsett picked up 18 yards and in the process passed Cornell's Ed Marinaro, the second leading rusher (4,715 yards) behind Ohio State's Archie Griffin (who has 5,177). Dorsett has 4,799.

When the drive stalled, Long kicked a 30-yard field goal for a 27-0 lead. It was on the

next series that Cavanaugh was injured at the end of a 5-yard gain. He was replaced by Migliore.

Yewcic then replaced Migliore near the end of the half and played the rest of the game despite a bruised right shoulder which he did not report until after the game.

Louisville received its first break when Wilbur Boggs intercepted Yewcic's deep pass near midfield and returned it to the 19, but the Cardinals were penalized to the 34 for clipping and the Pitt defense tightened up and didn't give up a yard.

The Panthers were barely able to make it to midfield the rest of the game, getting the ball in bad field position each time, and the offense went conservative to protect the lead, leaving it to the defense to do the rest.

Meanwhile, Bob Jury ended Louisville's only touchdown threat by intercepting a pass by Stram, the 5-8 son of the New Orleans Saints coach, Hank Stram, on the Pitt 13.

Louisville got its score when Mark Pangaonis blocked Swider's punt and Tom Abood recovered the ball in the end zone.

SCORE BY PERIODS

Louisville	0	0	0	6	–	6
Pitt	10	17	0	0	–	27

Before his injury, Cavanaugh scored 2 TD's for Pitt.

Pitt Zips to 'Greatest' Win, 36-19

By Russ Franke
Special to The Pittsburgh Press

Pittsburgh — "I wasn't around during the Jock Sutherland days," said Johnny Majors, "but I think this was Pitt's greatest win under the circumstances."

Majors was fairly gushing after his second-ranked Panthers ran their record to 6-0 with a 36-19 win over Miami at Pitt Stadium yesterday, a game that was full of question marks because of the quarterback "problem." It turned out that there was no problem after all.

The Panthers rallied behind their new quarterback, Tom Yewcic, and standing above them all was Tony Dorsett, who Majors said was "the greatest back I've ever seen, college or pro, on this day."

Dorsett gained 227 yards on 35 carries and scored three touchdowns, twice exploding on game-breaking plays. Going into next week's game at Navy, Dorsett needs but 152 yards to break the all-time rushing record of 5,177 yards by Ohio State's Archie Griffin.

Pitt ran up a 22-0 lead before Miami scored despite a conservative offense installed to protect Yewcic in his first start. Yewcic was called on to throw only seven passes and he completed two of them for 78 yards. Forty of those yards were pure Dorsett at his best, coming on a screen pass to the left in the second period for his second TD of the day. Dorsett reversed his field and ran away from everybody down the right sideline with the cuts and bursts of speed that are his trademark.

His first touchdown came on a 3-yard run and the third was a 53-yard blast through the middle that put the game away. Some of Dorsett's best gains came off the "I" formation, which the coaches installed this week to complement the Veer offense and make Yewcic's duties simpler.

"We went back to what we had been winning with for years — running the football," said Dorsett. "The 'I' is a good formation. I can explode in it."

Pitt's offensive line appeared to be at its best, putting out a special effort in a clutch situation.

Tony Dorsett's 227 yards and 3 TD's powered Pitt to a 6-0 record.

At center was John Pelusi, who missed last week's game with Louisville because of a bad knee. He was even more poetic than Majors afterward.

Majors merely called it "our finest hour." Pelusi said, "Love won today's game — love and togetherness. We knew what we had to do for the quarterback, and Tommy responded by

New Pitt quarterback Tom Yewcic turns the corner on a keeper play.

doing a helluva job. He had a sharp edge this week and we all knew it, and our fans were beautiful with all that noise."

Miami helped out Pitt in a critical game by losing five fumbles and throwing four interceptions, caused by a vicious Panther defense led by Al Romano, considered by many to be the best nose guard in the country. Romano had to leave in the fourth period with a pinched nerve in the neck but is expected to be ready next week. Pitt also lost fullback Elliott Walker temporarily because of dizziness after he had shown flashes of a return to form by gaining 54 yards on seven carries.

"We had that inner feeling we'd have to do a job today," said Romano. "They (the Miami backs) like to do a lot of show-boating and we had to rip into them."

Pitt rolled up 341 yards rushing while the defense held the Miami ground attack, led by Ottis (O.J.) Anderson and Ken Johnson, to 134. Miami's No. 1 quarterback, E.J. Baker, did not start because of a sprained wrist and played sparingly, completing only one pass.

The crowd of 42,434 did not know what to expect, having been led to believe that Pitt may not have been able to field a capable quarterback, but the enthusiasm from the stands for Dorsett and Yewcic grew as the games progressed. The Panthers, favored by two touchdowns, looked like winners from the start.

Majors kept the identity of his starting quarterback a secret, despite a story Thursday night that Yewcic had been told he would be the one. Majors and his QB coach, Bill Cox, also had freshman Woody Jackson and senior Dave Migliore ready.

"Five minutes before the game when I was warming up," said Yewcic, "Coach Majors asked me if I was ready to go and I said I'm as ready as I'll ever be, and he said, 'Good. You're starting.' Everybody's been behind Woody and me all week, and after our first offensive series, I knew we had it together."

Majors, looking like a new man after the ordeal of losing Matt Cavanaugh in last week's game with a fractured ankle (Pitt had lost its other experienced quarterback, Robert Haygood, in the second game), couldn't say enough for his coaching staff, Dorsett or Yewcic, who is now on scholarship after spending his previous three years as a practice field player.

"Under the circumstances, this was our toughest game," said Majors. "Our staff did the best job of planning for one game of any staff I've ever had. I bow very low to them. Tony Dorsett is a Heisman Trophy winner if I ever saw one, and I've never been prouder of a football player than I am of Tom Yewcic."

The Panther defense showed what kind of day it would be from the very start. After Dorsett had been stopped on the 1-yard line twice and Pitt gave up the ball, Leroy Felder burst through to nail Miami quarterback George

Mason in the end zone for two points.

Near the end of the first period, linebacker Arnie Weatherington recovered a ball knocked loose from fullback Ken Johnson on the Miami 30. Walker slammed through the left side with a pitchout to the 3 and Dorsett swept around the right side for a touchdown.

Felder again came through in the second period after Miami recovered Walker's fumble on the Pitt 14, intercepting in the end zone. Pitt marched back on Yewcic's 38-yard pass to tight end Jim Corbett at the Miami 15. Three plays gained only 5 yards and Carson Long kicked a 25-yard field goal.

Miami lost its third fumble, Bob Jury falling on Baker's muff on the Hurricane 24, and Long kicked another field goal, this one 39 yards. Long, incidentally, is having an excellent season, with seven field goals in 10 tries and a steady flow of kickoffs into the end zone.

Dorsett got his 101st yard of the day when he escaped 44 yards to the Miami 37 with time running out in the half. Pitt's momentum appeared to be stopped by an illegal motion penalty to the 40, but then came a bolt of Dorsett lightning — the 40-yard screen pass.

Miami made it 22-6 when Johnson powered 3 yards through the left side, and then Pitt got another break.

Larry Swider, the second leading punter in the nation, skied his shortest punt of the season, 26 yards. Eldridge Mitchell dropped the ball, however, and tackle George Messich recovered for Pitt on the Miami 32. Dorsett picked up 22 yards on a great cut and Yewcic ran 6 yards to the 7.

Then the Panthers got fancy, running a perfectly executed reverse from Yewcic to Dorsett to flanker Willie Taylor for a touchdown. Long's kick made it 29-6.

The Hurricanes' sub quarterback threw a 75-yard bomb to wingback Larry Cain for Miami's second score and Dorsett wiped that one out in a hurry. On the first play following the kickoff, Dorsett broke over the middle with a pitchout behind great blocking and raced 53 yards for a touchdown.

"Considering the position we were in today," said Majors, "Tony Dorsett had the greatest day of any back I've ever seen. He took the pressure off a new quarterback. Our defense was magnificent and this was a great day for Pitt football."

SCORE BY PERIODS

Miami	0	0	6	13	–	19
Pitt	9	13	0	14	–	36

Elliott Walker — the other back in Pitt's backfield — rushed for 54 yards against Miami.

Dorsett Sets Record, Pitt Romps

50

By Russ Franke
Special to The Pittsburgh Press

Annapolis, Md. — When Tony Dorsett does something, he does it in style.

The Pitt superstar knew he was being followed by a national television audience when the time came to make collegiate history.

In the fourth quarter of the Panthers' 45-0 rout of Navy, he needed but four yards to become the leading rusher in NCAA history.

With the ball on Navy's 32, Dorsett took a pitchout from Tom Yewcic, looked over the defense and blasted the record into oblivion by picking his way through the crowd for his third touchdown of the day. The run gave him 5,206 career yards, wiping out the record at 5,177 set last year by Ohio State's Archie Griffin.

With that, the entire Pitt bench erupted into a show of enthusiasm and raced onto the field to swallow up Dorsett, adding a mad fillip to their 45-0 rout of Nay.

The win, witnessed in person by only 26, 346 fans at Navy-Marine Corps Stadium, including some 5,000 Pitt followers, ran the second-ranked Panthers' record to 7-0. Dorsett carried the ball 27 times for 180 yards (he needed 152) and his career total carries also broke the record of 918 held by Cornell's Ed Marinaro.

Meanwhile, the Pitt defense held Navy to only 106 yards in total offense. Yewcic started his second game at quarterback for Pitt and completed eight of 10 passes for 97 yards and one TD in an offense geared to Dorsett.

It didn't take the Panthers long to score after the defense stopped Navy at midfield on the first series. Navy punted short to the Panther 26 and Dorsett, Yewcic and tight end Jim Corbett combined to move in on a 74-yard march using the "I" formation.

Dorsett picked up 23 yards on five carries and a 19-yard pass to Corbett moved the sticks to the Navy 41. With the Navy defense playing Dorsett tight two plays later, Yewcic flipped a quick pass to Corbett cutting across the middle and Corbett went all the way behind the blocking for a 30-yard touchdown, and Carson Long's kick gave Pitt a 7-0 lead midway through

---

Tony Dorsett's fourth-quarter 32-yard TD run set a new NCAA rushing record.

the first period.

Dorsett ran for gains of 10, 15 and 6 yards on the next series but the drive stalled on the Navy 39 and Larry Swider punted to the end zone.

The Panthers were set up for another score early in the second quarter when Dorsett ripped off 12 yards and Yewcic passed 14 yards to Willie Taylor on the Navy 27, but the Panthers couldn't get another first down and Long's 42-yard field goal try was wide.

An alert play by George O'Korn gave Pitt another chance, but once again the Navy defense held and Long's 49-yard field goal attempt was short. The chance came when a Navy punt hit a teammate, John Sturgoss, and O'Korn recovered the ball on the Navy 24.

Navy was barely able to move out of its own territory in the first half with a great deal of pressure exerted on quarterback Bob Lesczcynski and a solid front wall thrown up against the run by Randy Holloway, Al Romano and Don Parrish.

With time running out in the half, Pitt struck suddenly for another score. With Navy deep in the hole, Panther end Cecil Johnson blocked Art Ohanian's punt at the 10 and Romano fell on the ball on the 6.

On the next play, Dorsett took Yewcic's pitchout to the left behind a wall of blockers and Dorsett made it in for a touchdown easily. Long's conversion made it 14-0.

For the half, Dorsett totaled 71 yards on 14 carries.

On the first series following intermission,

52

Tony Dorsett (above) rambles for short yardage. Jim Corbett (right) scores on a 30-yard pass in the first quarter.

Dorsett broke Marinaro's NCAA record for running attempts with the 919th carry of his career.

After Swider punted to the end zone when the series died, Navy tried to move out of the hole by passing and Leroy Felder picked off Lescycnski's throw and returned 4 yards to the Navy 29. The Panthers were unable to get a first down, however, and Long was true with a 40-yard field goal, his sixth of the year in 10 attempts, increasing the lead to 17-0.

Holloway, Parrish, Romano & Co. continued to terrorize the Navy offense into punting situations, and after Ohanian kicked to the Pitt 26, lightning struck from a source other than Dorsett. After Dorsett gained 5 yards to bring the day's total to 94, fullback Elliott Walker broke through the right side and rambled 69 yards for a touchdown, outracing the Navy secondary. Long's kick ran the score to 24-0.

Pitt marched 47 yards for its next score and in the process Dorsett raced past the 100-yard total for the 15th straight game. He ended the drive with a 21-yard scoring run when he banged through the middle, broke a tackle and dived over the goal line.

Also in the process he became the first player in NCAA history to gain 1,000 yard four straight years.

The drama, already building in the press box, where Dorsett's log was being kept and announced, reached its peak when Dorsett needed but 4 yards to break the record with the ball on the Navy 32.

He took a pitchout left from Yewcic and ripped around the left side, dancing behind his blockers and made it all the way in for his third touchdown of the day.

The Pitt bench also had been informed of Dorsett's figures and when Dorsett was swarmed by his blockers in the end zone, the entire Pitt bench poured onto the field to celebrate. The Panthers were breaking the rules, but they didn't care. They were on national television and history was being made.

The TD run, with 13:22 left in the game, was his 27th carry of the day. When Long kicked the point, it was 38-0.

The Panthers scored their last touchdown with 51 seconds remaining, behind the quarterbacking of freshman Woody Jackson, when Thom Sindewald powered 16 yards through center.

55

SCORE BY PERIODS

Pitt	7	7	10	21	–	45
Navy	0	0	0	0	–	0

Pitt's J.C. Wilson piles up Navy tailback Joe Gattuso.

National Championship Team Made 1936 a Golden Year

By Bill Modoono
The Pittsburgh Press

Pittsburgh, Oct. 26, 1986 — Those were the days, all right. The days when the Rose Bowl was merely "the Daddy of postseason battles." The days when sportswriters could get away with describing halfbacks as running "with all the abandon of a typhoon on holiday." The days when a game between Holy Cross and Temple could help determine the matchups of the New Year's Day bowls.

Great days, they were. Why back in 1936, you could be No. 3 in The Associated Press, No. 2 in Pittsburgh and still wind up No. 1 in the nation.

It happened to Pitt. Its 1936 football team won the Rose Bowl and was generally recognized as the national champion, despite having lost, 7-0, to Duquesne.

Duquesne, incidentally, defeated Mississippi State in the Orange Bowl that season. Yep, those were the days.

Pitt honored its 1936 team on its 50th anniversary this weekend. Conveniently, the 50th anniversary of the team that won the only Rose Bowl in Pitt history coincides with the university's bicentennial celebration.

Back for the ceremonies were such fabled names as "Mad" Marshall Goldberg, Bobby LaRue and Harold "Curly" Stebbins. Certainly mentioned about 1,000 times during the weekend was the name of Jock Sutherland, Pitt's legendary coach.

The men doing the talking were in their 70's, but when mention is made of "the old man," everyone knew the subject of the conversation.

No player ever called Sutherland that to his face, however. "We always called him Doctor," said Bill Daddio, a two-way sophomore end for the 1936 team.

Pitt assistant Bill Kern and Jock Sutherland on the sideline in 1936.

"Jock Sutherland was very demanding," said LaRue, a senior halfback in 1936. "If something wasn't done exactly his way ... Of course, his way was the best way."

That fact was confirmed in 1936, 1937 and 1938, when Pitt had a combined record of 25-3-2. It also was proven in 1939, when Sutherland left and Pitt slumped to a 5-4 record and then went eight years before having another winning season.

"Every new coach that comes to Pitt — Johnny Majors, Jackie Sherrill, Mike Gottfried — always seems to talk about Pitt's 'football tradition,' " said Ave Daniell, an all-American tackle and senior captain in 1936. "I think they're missing one word. It should be Pitt's 'winning football tradition.' In the four years I was at the school, the most games we ever lost in one season was one."

The 1936 team was an important one in Pitt history, first for the Rose Bowl title that it won (21-0 against Washington) and for the all-Americans it produced (six players from that team earned such recognition in their careers, two of them twice). But 1936 also was the beginning of the end of Pitt's 14-year connection with Sutherland.

Sutherland's dissatisfaction with the Pitt administration came to a head in Pasadena, Calif. A dispute over how much spending money the players were entitled to have on the West Coast created enough ill will to convince

Anatomy of the Season

How Pitt fared against opponents in the 1936 national championship season when it compiled an 8-1-1 record.

Game	Pitt	Opp.
Ohio Wesleyan	53	0
West Virginia	34	0
at Ohio State	6	0
at Duquesne	0	7
Notre Dame	26	0
at Fordham	0	0
Penn State	24	7
at Nebraska	19	6
Carnegie Tech	31	14
Washington (Rose Bowl)	21	0

the players to vote down a return trip to the Rose Bowl following a 9-0-1 season in 1937.

By then, most of the nation was convinced of Pitt's excellence, but the matter was not as simple in 1936. Victories against Ohio Wesleyan (53-0), West Virginia (34-0) and Ohio State (6-0) were impressive, but inconclusive. Things looked especially bleak when Pitt was defeated by Duquesne the following week.

"We were just cocky and they had a darned good football team," Daniell said.

The loss to Duquesne was so bitter that one

Pitt player, George Musulin, reportedly told Sutherland, "I'm so mad about losing to Duquesne that I'm going to stop drinkin' that Duquesne beer."

According to Daniell, Sutherland did not attend practice for three days after the Duquesne loss, which further increased the anxiety of the players. "We were scared to death," Daniell said.

So scared that the team rebounded to rout Notre Dame, 26-0, and put itself back in the race for national recognition. The only other blemish on the record was a 0-0 tie with Fordham and its legendary "Seven Blocks of Granite" at the Polo Grounds.

"At no time did the backfields outshine the rushlines," wrote Chester Smith in The Pittsburgh Press account of the game. "Next year, they are going to start the game on Monday morning and keep at it until somebody scores."

With the tie and the loss to Duquesne on the record and an 0-3 record in previous Rose Bowls, Pitt was not a popular choice to represent the East in Pasadena on Jan. 1, 1937. "The newspaper publicity was all anti-Pitt," Daniell said. "Why pick Pitt to go? they asked. But we were a good team that year with players who had the makings of a great team."

The 1936 team had only three senior starters — Daniell, LaRue and Bill Glassford. Included on the team were John Chickerneo, Stebbins and Goldberg, who would be celebrated in 1938

Jock Sutherland posted a record of 111-20-12 and won 5 national championships at Pitt.

as part of Pitt's legendary "Dream Backfield."

Steve Petro was a third-string sophomore guard when the train left Pittsburgh for California Dec. 15, 1936. By New Year's Day, he had become a starter.

"It took us three night and two days to get out there," Petro recalled. "And we stopped and practiced in Albuquerque."

Sutherland instituted two-a-day practices before the Rose Bowl and even went so far as to bring bottled water from Pittsburgh. Petro's work in practice earned him the promotion to first team.

The extended time in California was tough on the players, financially. Sutherland wanted the administration to give the 33-member squad meal money, but the request was denied. According to Petro, Daniell and Daddio, Sutherland wound up taking money out of his own pocket to pay the players.

"We got about $7 each," Daniell said.

"The seniors got more," Petro said. "I got $3.60. When I came back from California, I wound up owing $80 that I borrowed."

The star of the game was Daddio, who kicked three conversions and intercepted a lateral and ran 70 yards for a touchdown.

"The funny thing was I had done the same thing in practice," Daddio said. "The second team ran the Washington offense and I intercepted a lateral then, too."

"When the white shirts start running," wrote

Smith of the Pitt team, "they are pure cussedness on wheels."

The Rose Bowl victory earned Pitt the national championship according to both the *Illustrated Football Annual* and the *Football Thesaurus*. The AP, in its first season of ranking teams, listed Pitt No. 3.

"The value of a national championship was minimized in those days," Daniell said. "There was no way someone from the East could know how good a Nebraska was or a Washington. The Eastern championship, the Lambert trophy, the Big Ten, and the Pac-8 titles — those were the ones that mattered then."

Although Daniell, Goldberg, Daddio, Glassford, Frank Souchak and Tony Matisi were recognized as all-Americans and Goldberg was a runner-up in a Heisman Trophy balloting, Petro remembers the 1936 team as one "without any stars."

That could be because there was so much balance. Or it could mean Sutherland dominated the team. "He taught and believed that no one man was better than another," said Petro of the coach the newspapers referred to as "The Dour Scot."

"He would tell us that the man opposite you was only as tough as you let him be."

"I don't think he ever got to know his players well," Daddio said. "He avoided that. He was very strict, he worked you hard, but he was very fair."

"There was a joke we used to tell about the

"The players were very much afraid of him," Daniell said. "Most didn't like him and were scared to death of him."

"But he was an advocate of detail, a fundamental football man. He taught you well, that's why lots of his players became coaches themselves."

Sutherland did not believe in any drill that was not related directly to football, such as wind sprints. Instead of wind sprints, his teams ran signal drills in formations up and down the field.

"If he saw an opponent do something well, he'd use it," Petro said.

"Penn State ran the sneak well against us, then we added the 'Penn State sneak' to our playbook. He was always looking to learn something about football."

The next season, despite rejecting bowl invitations, AP voted Pitt No. 1 again. In March of 1939, Sutherland reluctantly resigned in the face of what appeared to be a growing de-emphasis at Pitt. The next day, the students struck in protest. They must have known something. Pitt would not win another national championship until 1976.

"We went to Pitt in those days expecting to be winners," Daniell said. "We never even thought about losing."

Doctor," Petro said. "One guy would say he just had a long conversation with him. Another player would ask, 'What'd he say?' The other would reply, 'Hello.' "

Jock Sutherland and his Dream Backfield of the late 1930's.

Pitt Stone-walls Syracuse, 23-13

62

BY RUSS FRANKE
Special to The Pittsburgh Press

Pittsburgh — Pitt can be thankful for Joe Stone's keen set of ears and Tony Dorsett's magic set of legs.

They were two of the factors that helped keep the Panthers unbeaten yesterday in their toughest game of the season, and it wasn't until the final minute that they were able to escape the clutches of fired-up Syracuse.

As usual in the Pitt-Syracuse series, bodies flew all over the field, and after the last one had fallen, Pitt had a 23-13 win and was glad to get out alive.

Syracuse sprang a sophomore quarterback named Bill Hurley on the Panthers and he happened to be the best young quarterback Pitt coach Johnny Majors said he has seen in years. Hurley broke the school record for total offense with 303 yards and gave the Pitt secondary its roughest day of the season with his passing on the run.

Only the hard hitting of the Pitt defense, which knocked loose two fumbles, an interception by Bob Jury and a sensational defensive stand near the end deprived the Orangemen of near-certain chances for four more scores.

The defensive stand at the Pitt 11-yard line late in the fourth period is where Stone's ears entered the dramatic picture. He recognized an audible call by Hurley as one he had heard moments earlier, and when the Orangemen ran their fullback into the line, Stone and his mates were waiting for him.

Pitt had a shaky 20-13 lead and Syracuse had third-and-1 to go on the 11. Jim Sessler hit the middle and was stopped two inches short of the sticks. On the next play, the Panthers knew Sessler was coming again and tackle Don Parrish stood him upright and linebacker Arnie Weatherington kept him from bending forward in a fierce pileup.

Syracuse coach Frank Maloney ran onto the

Joe Stone (above) was the hero of the game for Pitt. (Right) Arnie Weatherington (59) and Al Romano (91) crush Syracuse quarterback Bill Hurley.

field to protest the marking of the ball and drew a 15-yard penalty, and the Panthers were out of the hole with just over three minutes to play.

Dorsett then took command and ripped off gains of 28 and 33 yards to ensure possession, and with the ball on the Syracuse 12, Carson Long kicked his third field goal of the day to put the game away.

"It was surely a game of breaks," said Majors. "We were awfully good to them on our handling of the kickoffs, which was stupid.

"Number 33 (Dorsett) came through again when we really needed him, coming back after that injury. To be a winner, you have to win the close games — they all won't be walkaways.

"It wasn't really a bad day for us. Syracuse just did a good job of preparing. That young quarterback moved the ball on us but our defense was still great in the clutch."

The injury Majors spoke of came in the first half when Dorsett heard his elbow pop and thought it was broken. Dorsett was hit even though he didn't have the ball.

"That's the way it happened up at Syracuse two years ago, the only serious injury I've ever had," said Dorsett.

He was forced out yesterday three times with various injuries, none serious, and neither of his two running mates, Elliott Walker and Bob-

by Hutton, finished the game. Walker went out with two-sprained ankles and Hutton with a shoulder injury.

Syracuse's outstanding monster back, Larry King, also was forced out with a concussion when Gordon Jones delivered a sharp crack-back block in one of the hardest-hitting games of the Pitt season.

"I don't know how they lost four games, the way they played today," Pitt nose guard Al Romano said of the team from his hometown. "Their quarterback ran better than I thought he would, but the biggest surprise was his passing."

Hurley, often throwing while being chased, completed nine of 18 passes for 203 yards. One of his passes, an 80-yarder to wingback Don Magee, which caught the Pitt secondary flat-footed, went down as the longest scoring throw in Syracuse history.

Tom Yewcic, Pitt's emergency quarterback, threw only seven passes and completed two, as the Panthers relied mainly on the running backs coming off the "I" formation.

Dorsett carried 34 times for 241 yards, his greatest output of the season, to pass another record. He broke Archie Griffin's all-time major college record in last week's 45-0 win over Navy. And yesterday he passed Howard Stevens' all-college record of 5,297 yards set at

Tony Dorsett dances into the end zone after a 32-yard TD run.

Randolph-Macon and Louisville.

It was Dorsett's 16th straight 100-yard plus game and he now has gained 5,447 yards in his career.

Syracuse showed little respect for the Pitt defense, rated fourth in the country, from the start, marching to the Pitt 8 on the first series. Fullback Earl Vaughn had the ball torn away from him, however, and Cecil Johnson recovered the fumble.

Pitt got its first score when Carson Long kicked the first of his three field goals that proved to be invaluable in the end. This one was a 41-yarder that was set up when Yewcic threw a quickie pass to tight end Jim Corbett for 23 yards, gains of 8 and 10 yards by Walker and Willie Taylor's flanker pass to Corbett for 11.

The Orangemen took a 7-3 lead with the bomb to Magee near the end of the first period, and the crowd of 50,399 began to get worried.

Dorsett got himself into gear on Pitt's next series, a 95-yard march, breaking tackles and dancing for gains of 33 and 15 yards. Hutton, spelling Walker, also pitched in with a gain of 8 to the 2. Dorsett had to hit the line twice for a touchdown.

Syracuse threatened again, getting to the 6, where Vaughn was hit hard in the middle and fumbled. Ed Wilamowski recovered for Pitt.

Early in the third period, Syracuse tied it at 10-10 on Dave Jacobs' 45-yard field goal. Jacobs then kicked a 55-yarder for a 13-10 lead and a Pitt Stadium record.

Pitt clawed from behind with an 80-yard drive, Yewcic getting a key first down with a 4-yard run on fourth-and-1 at the Syracuse 33. On the next play Dorsett took a pitchout and with the aid of Corbett's block, raced all the way.

The lead went up to 20-13 early in the fourth quarter after Syracuse was called for pass interference and Yewcic ran for 13 and 7 yards to set up a 47-yard field goal by Long.

Again Syracuse threatened, with Hurley getting away for 15 yards and Pitt getting nailed for a face-mask penalty. With the ball on the Pitt 21, safetyman Bob Jury leaped in front of Hurley's receiver for an interception to kill another threat.

The Orangemen still had some fight, forcing a punt by Larry Swider and bringing the ball back into position for a possible go-ahead touchdown. It was here that Stone, primarily an offensive tackle, came in to bolster the defensive line in its furious stand at the 11.

Dorsett ensured Pitt's eighth win of the year by tearing away on dodging runs of 28 and 33 yards, setting up a 29-yard field goal by Long with 27 seconds left.

SCORE BY PERIODS

Syracuse	7	0	6	0	–	13
Pitt	3	7	7	6	–	23

67

After the go-ahead TD, Dorsett is mobbed by his teammates in the end zone.

Panthers Cry 'No.1,' Beat Army

68

BY RUSS FRANKE
Special to The Pittsburgh Press

Pittsburgh — "It's gonna be hard to beat the University of Pittsburgh from here on out," said Tony Dorsett, adding the exclamation point to a dramatic day for Pitt football.

Dorsett had just exploded for 212 yards to add some trimming to his record as college football's all-time leading rusher before getting knocked out of action at the start of the fourth quarter in the Panthers' 37-7 romp over Army yesterday. Then the news of Purdue's 16-14 upset over top-ranked Michigan blared out of the public address system and Dorsett and his teammates on the sidelines danced gleefully as the homecoming crowd of 45,573 roared, "We're Number One!"

Second ranked with an 8-0 record going into the Army game, the Panthers are now one win away from the most in Pitt history. Should they get it next Saturday at home against West Virginia, they will be able to name their preference in bowl games.

Someone asked Johnny Majors if he thought Pitt was No. 1, and he said, "There's no doubt in my mind. With this team, I'd take my chances with anybody. But it's nothing to sit on — we've still got to claw and scratch and block and tackle when we play West Virginia."

The uproarious afternoon for Pitt also was marked by the return of the Matt Cavanaugh to quarterback. Cavanaugh, who had been out for a month recovering from an ankle fracture, relieved starter Tom Yewcic in the first period with Pitt ahead, 3-0, on Carson Long's 27-yard field goal.

Someone in the media noted, "Yewcic thus retires as the only undefeated quarterback in college football history."

"Tom Yewcic did a fine job for three weeks when we needed him," said Majors. "But Cavanaugh picked us up and loosened up Army because they have to respect his arm. Matt is going to become one of the outstanding quarterbacks in the country. I wouldn't trade him for anybody as a leading quarterback.

"Still, both Matt and Tom are green shirts

After defeating Army, 37-7, Bobby Hutton (44) celebrates Pitt's new No. 1 ranking.

(the first-team offense wears green in practice)."

While Dorsett was high-stepping to another Heisman Trophy-type day, the Pitt defense had very little trouble handling Army quarterback Leamon Hall.

Hall came into the game as the nation's sixth-leading passer, but he was intercepted three times in the first half — by Jeff Delaney, Leroy Felder and Bob Jury, the safety who is among the country's leaders in interceptions with seven.

The front wall of Al Romano, Randy Holloway, Don Parrish, Cecil Johnson and Ed Wilamowski also shut down Army's ground game (78 yards and three first downs).

"It was difficult for us to play a team like Pittsburgh," said Army coach Homer Smith. "We simply took a beating. Of course I feel Pitt should be No. 1.

"The speed of Tony Dorsett is unbelievable when you watch it from the field. I don't know how it looks from upstairs. He is unquestionably the fastest running back who ever played the game."

Dorsett's 212 yards ran his career rushing total to 5,659 and gave him 1,525 for the season. He is the first one in NCAA history with three 1,500-yard seasons.

Dorsett also scored three of Pitt's four touchdowns. Going in, he led the nation in points

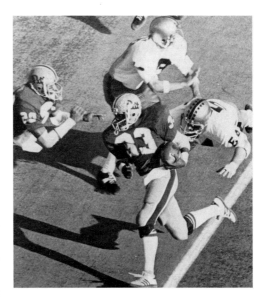

with a total of 86.

He still has a shot at 6,000 yards for a career, a feat once believed impossible. He needs 341 yards in the remaining games with West Virginia and Penn State.

"I'm not shooting for 6,000," said Dorsett, in his post-game press conference. "My goal is to be the national champs. I've accomplished every personal goal I set before the season. Whatever else happens is icing on the cake."

With fullback Elliott Walker out of action because of an ankle sprain, Pitt received some

Tony Dorsett (33) rushed for 212 yards and scored three touchdowns against Army.

running support from Thom Sindewald, with 64 yards on 10 carries up the middle. Cavanaugh also chipped in with 76 yards rushing while hitting eight of 12 passes, one of them a 24-yarder to flanker Willie Taylor for a touchdown.

"I felt a little rusty in the warmup," said Cavanaugh. "But the ankle is getting stronger every day. It's not sore at all now."

On the first play of the game, the Pitt defense was waiting for Hall, Delaney dropping off along the sideline to steal a deep throw, and the Cadets couldn't get a thing going until the score was 27-0.

Felder's interception came near the end of the first period, setting up Long's field goal. He was to kick a total of three — of 37, 27 and 35 yards — giving him 15 of 21 for the season in addition to 36-for-36 in extra points.

The Panthers marched 64 yards for Long's next field goal and they got their first touchdown just before halftime with an 88-yard drive. Meanwhile, Dorsett passed Archie Griffin's

Carson Long booted 3 field goals — 37, 27 and 35 yards — in defeating the Cadets.

all-time career record of 6,003 yards in all-purpose running, a category that includes returns and pass interceptions.

Dorsett, Sindewald and versatile Bobby Hutton got most of the yardage on the march, and Dorsett ended it by smacking through the middle for a 4-yard touchdown.

On their first series of the second half, the Panthers went 76 yards, and in the process, Dorsett reached 100 yards for the 17th straight game. Cavanaugh ran for a pair of first downs and when the ball was at the Army 32, Dorsett picked out a hole, changed speeds and raced inside the left pylon.

Pitt made it 27-0 on its next possession, which lasted just 51 seconds. Cavanaugh escaped 49 yards to the 5 and Dorsett swept the left side cleanly with a pitchout.

Army broke through after Greg King got into the open on a reverse for 40 yards. The score came when Hall passed 27 yards to tight end Mark Logue, who juggled the ball and dived into the end zone.

Cavanaugh whipped a pass over the middle to Taylor behind nice blocking for another touchdown and Long completed the scoring with his 35-yard field goal at the end of a drive quarterbacked by freshman Woody Jackson.

Pitt No. 1, First Time Since 1937

The weekly rankings in college football announced by both wire services today confirmed what delirious Pitt fans have believed since last Saturday — the Panthers are No. 1 in the nation.

Pitt's 37-7 victory over Army, running its record to 9-0 for the season, coupled with previously top-ranked Michigan's 16-14 upset loss to Purdue, shot Pitt to No. 1 for the first time since 1937, when the first wire service poll of sportswriters and broadcasters was taken. In 1937, Pitt compiled a record of nine wins, no losses and a tie and finished the season No. 1.

The current Panther team has two regular-season games remaining in which to protect and maintain its top ranking and receive a major bowl invitation to either the Orange Bowl or Sugar Bowl on New Year's Day. The remaining two games on the regular schedule are with West Virginia on Saturday at Pitt Stadium and with Penn State on Friday night, Nov. 26, at Three Rivers Stadium.

Both games are sold out, but will be televised.

SCORE BY PERIODS

Army	0	0	7	0	–	7
Pitt	3	10	21	3	–	37

The Passing of the Torch: Goldberg to Dorsett

By Phil Axelrod
Special to The Post-Gazette

Pittsburgh, Nov. 11, 1976 — Pacing the sideline at every Pitt football game wearing a bright blue and gold windbreaker is Steve Petro, the first to congratulate a player coming off the field.

After every Tony Dorsett touchdown, Petro is there to greet him with a hug and a pat on the rump. For 40 years, Petro, now the assistant to the athletic director, has had an unfaltering love affair with Pitt's football program.

That affair traces back to the glory days of 1937 when he was a sturdy two-way guard for Dr. John Bain (Jock) Sutherland's national championship Panthers.

The 1976 Panthers, 9-0 and ranked No. 1, are on the verge of becoming Pitt's first national champion since the all-purpose Marshall (Biggie) Goldberg led the '37 Panthers to a 9-0-1 record, the tie being the third in a memorable series of 0-0 standoffs with Fordham.

The other day when Petro picked up the newspaper to verify that the AP and UPI polls had indeed picked the Panthers No. 1 he was hit by a wave of nostalgia and warm memories.

"We used to do that in '37," he said, running his hand through a gray, one-inch high brush cut. "It gave us the same kind of excitement then."

During a midweek lull awaiting Pitt's game against arch-rival West Virginia this Saturday at Pitt Stadium, Petro was inundated by misty-eyed memories. Of Goldberg, of Dr. Sutherland, of Pitt football.

"To this day, I can't call him Jock," Petro said of the stern Sutherland, who coached the Panthers from 1924 to 1938.

Petro fondly calls him "Dr. Sutherland" out of respect and admiration for the man who molded Pitt's football program with an iron hand.

Marshall (Biggie) Goldberg — all-America (1937, 1938) and Heisman Trophy runner-up.

"He wasn't so much mean, but more all business," Petro said. "He demanded so much from every athlete."

Petro thought a second, then added, "His demands were that you were the best that you could be. He never wasted a moment since practices were business, time to learn what you were expected to do in a game."

Those Pitt teams rang up a 25-3-2 record while Petro was there. The 1937 champs outscored opponents, 203-94.

Leading Pitt's attack was Goldberg, a true all-America who held the school's career rushing mark of 1,957 yards until Dorsett ran right past it in the second game of his sophomore season. Dorsett has gone on to rush for 5,659 yards and is nearing the mythical 6,000-mark.

But oldtimers still insist that Biggie Goldberg was the greatest who ever lived. Petro, who has seen them both, was asked the question: "Who was better, Goldberg or Dorsett?"

Petro smiled knowingly. He's answered it often, and was willing to give it another try. "Tony Dorsett is as good a runner as Goldberg," he said, "but Goldberg was a great defensive back and I haven't seen Dorsett play defense."

Not trying to cop out, Petro pointed out that back in '37 the players went both ways, whereas today the game has become more specialized

and requires a player to have more adept skills.

"It's not fair to make comparisons," he added with a grin that broke into a smile all over his face. "You were called on to do more things in 60 minutes back then. After 59 minutes of football, there's no way Goldberg could be as fast as

Steve Petro, a long-time assistant at Pitt, was a teammate of Marshall Goldberg.

Goldberg-Dorsett Breakdown

Category	Goldberg	Dorsett
All-America	1937, 1938	1973, 1974, 1975, 1976
Heisman	1938 runner-up	1976 winner
Rushing yardage	1,957 yards	6,626 yards

Dorsett in his final minute."

The 1937 team had nine starters who played offense and defense.

"If you played two-way you were more experienced about what the offense and the defense did so you were a more complete football player," Petro said, leaning back in his chair with a faraway look in his eyes. "You could appreciate the offensive and defensive problems."

Giving the 1976 team credit without trying to compare the two, Petro said, "This team has more depth."

If — and it's a hypothetical if because there's no way it can happen — the '37 Panthers played the '76 Panthers, who would win?

"You can't say," Petro answered. "I would say for a quarter the '37 team could stay with them."

Petro then laughed. "This is the best Pitt squad since 1937," he said. "The results are similar. The greatest feeling for me is to see that they're doing so well, if not better than we did."

Thinking back just a few years ago when the Panthers floundered around with three consecutive 1-9 seasons under Dave Hart, Petro said, "There were times when I thought I'd never again see a Pitt team No. 1."

Needless to say, if it weren't for Dorsett, Pitt wouldn't be there now.

"You need a guy like that to be No. 1," Petro said. "We had Goldberg."

Without getting too gushy, Petro explained the feeling he has every time he watches this Pitt team win a football game.

"There's no one more proud of the University of Pittsburgh that I am," he said with sincerity. "Anybody who has been a Pitt man has to be elated."

Particularly a Pitt man for 40 years who was a member of another No. 1 Pitt team in another era.

"It's like reliving an experience," he said. "You can't put it into words."

Panthers Hold Off WVU, 24-16

By Russ Franke
Special to The Pittsburgh Press

Pittsburgh — Tony Dorsett raised his finger to the West Virginia bench before the game and waved goodbye to the crowd before it was over. What happened in between, however, was what counted yesterday when Pitt and West Virginia tried to blast each other out of Pitt Stadium.

Pitt managed to survive five lost fumbles and Dorsett banged home three more touchdowns and when it was all over but the fighting, the Panthers were still undefeated and presumably still No. 1 in the nation with a 24-16 win.

If the zany series needed any more spice, it was supplied in the final minute when Dorsett was kicked out of the game for fighting after a late hit. The hit was late by 199 yards, which is what Dorsett gained on 38 carries, the high for his career.

The Panthers had the game locked away with 22 seconds remaining and the sellout crowd of 56,500 and a regional television audience were deliberating whether Pitt will take the Sugar Bowl or the Orange Bowl. Then Dorsett was hit in front of the Pitt bench and came up swinging, slamming the ball into Robin Meeley's helmet. Both teams milled around before Dorsett was ejected.

"I'm a man and a human being, and I can only take so much," said Dorsett later, "then emotion takes over, especially in a game like this.

"I was getting a lot of dirty play laid on me throughout the ball game and I was overlooking it. It was obvious to me he tried to spear me when I was down — he went for my head.

"I don't mind getting hit, but they were going for my eyes.

"It was a helluva ball game, though, like we expected when Pitt and West Virginia get together."

If Dorsett took a sound beating, quarterback Matt Cavanaugh took an even worse one. He was knocked out of action briefly in the third quarter but returned and finished with his best rushing day ever. The Mountaineers knocked

Tony Dorsett scored on a 2-yard TD run in the second quarter.

the ball away from him three times, but Cavanaugh still gained 124 yards.

"West Virginia was giving me the run on the option — they just didn't want Tony carrying the ball — so I took it. They hit the hell out of me. Now I know how Tony feels, the way he takes a beating all the time. I have more respect for him than ever."

Unable to run against the difficult Pitt front wall, the Mountaineers had to go to the air for both of their touchdowns, Dan Kendra to wide receiver Steve Lewis for 14 and 9 yards.

The second one made a real dogfight of what up to then had been a mere scrap. It ended the scoring with just over three minutes left, and the Panthers ran out the clock.

"I am darn glad to get out of the game with a victory," said Johnny Majors. "Eight points isn't that big of a margin (Pitt was favored by more than three touchdowns) but I'll take it in a game like this any day. Both teams were sky high and played with a lot of pride.

"I have nothing but the utmost respect for how Frank Cignetti prepared his team. But we hurt ourselves a lot with mistakes and just bad execution, and part of this was caused by West Virginia's aggressiveness on defense."

Pitt's defense showed its teeth early, stopping WVU cold on the first two series, and

the second time the Panthers got the ball they drove 68 yards. Dorsett did most of the carrying, and there was a 9-yard pass from Cavanaugh to Jim Corbett and with the ball on the WVU 17, Dorsett jitterbugged off the right side and escaped down the sideline for a touchdown. Carson Long, the leading kick-scorer for a career in NCAA history, kicked the point after.

In the fourth quarter, Dorsett came up swinging after a late hit.

West Virginia cut the lead to 7-3 when Randy Weppler recovered a fumble on the Pitt 22 and Bill McKenzie, who won last year's game in Morgantown with a field goal, kicked one from 22 yards out.

Pitt, which surprisingly had opened the game with three pass plays, stuck to the ground for its next touchdown, a march of 69 yards.

Cavanaugh displayed some remarkable running ability on the series, picking his way through for gains of 17, 9 and 20 yards. Bobby Hutton, subbing at fullback for the injured Elliott Walker for the second straight week, gained 3 yards, while Dorsett squeezed out gains of 6 and 3 yards to the 2. From there, Dorsett punched through the middle for a touchdown and Long made it 14-3, early in the second period.

West Virginia had a shot with time running out in the half when Chuck Smith recovered Cavanaugh's fumble at the Pitt 43, but cornerback J.C. Wilson got the ball back by intercepting Kendra's pass on Pitt's 32.

The Panthers had something going on their first possession of the second half when Cavanaugh got loose for 15 and 12 yards. Corbett caught a 10-yard pass on the 10 but had to settle for Long's 27-yard field goal, his 15th in 21 tries this year and 249th point of his career.

Dorsett scored 3 TD's against West Virginia.

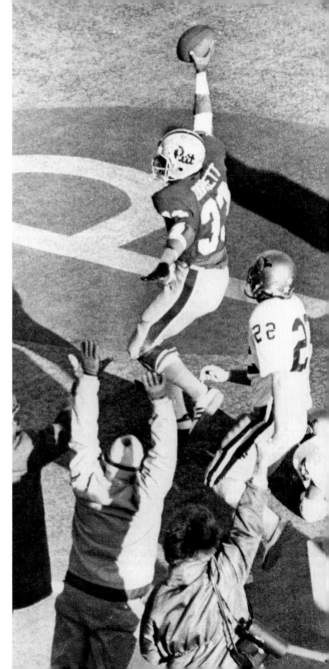

Fumbles continued to plague Pitt in the third period, and the Mountaineers pulled the ball loose from Cavanaugh and Ken Culbertson recovered for WVU on his 43.

Kendra passed 10 and 17 yards to Lewis and although Randy Holloway sacked Kendra for 8 yards, Kendra found Lewis in a crowd in the end zone on a 14-yard throw.

Cavanaugh, bruised on the right elbow and shoulder, had to be replaced by Tom Yewcic for two series, and after Dorsett tore off 20 yards on four carries, Hutton gained 5 and Yewcic 12 to midfield. Cavanaugh returned to finish off the drive of 87 yards.

The drive was kept alive when West Virginia was caught clipping on Larry Swider's punt to the 1, resulting in a first down on the 31. Dorsett carried for just 1 yard but on the next play, he drove the crowd wild and West Virginia crazy.

Dorsett took a pitchout to the left and appeared to be hemmed in, but he went to the afterburner and raced down the sideline 30 yards for a touchdown, breaking tackles by Tom Pridemore and Paul Jordan. Long's 39th extra point in 39 tries this season made it 24-10.

The scrappy Mountaineers weren't through by any means. Fullback Walt Easley, doing a good job replacing the injured Paul Lumley, got away for 17 yards following Macerelli's recovery of a Cavanaugh fumble on the Pitt 34.

Easley, Dwayne Woods and Kendra took turns carrying to the 8. Leroy Felder and Bob Jury made what appeared to be a drive-stopping play by nailing Woods on the 9, but on third and goal, Kendra threw to Lewis in heavy traffic at the goal line to make it 24-16. Kendra's two-point pass attempt was out of the end zone.

Shortly afterward, the fight started and the game ended, the Panthers had the most wins of any team in Pitt history.

Dorsett now has 5,858 yards for his career and a jersey all his own. At halftime, Majors and Athletic Director Cas Myslinski gave him a jersey numbered 33, the first time a jersey has been retired in Pitt's 86 years of football.

SCORE BY PERIODS

West Virginia	3	0	7	6	–	16
Pitt	7	7	3	7	–	24

The retirement of Dorsett's jersey (33) was the first ever in Pitt history.

Panthers Claw Nittany Lions, 24-7

By Marino Parascenzo
Special to The Post-Gazette

Pittsburgh — The Pitt Panthers last night gave Johnny Majors a good reason for returning to Tennessee. On the other hand, they gave him a good reason for staying.

Majors at last knows that Pitt can beat the Penn State Nittany Lions.

The Panthers whipped the Lions, 24-7, behind a brilliant, 224-yard record-setting performance by Heisman Trophy candidate Tony Dorsett.

It had been getting to the point that the Panthers had to wonder whether they could ever beat the Lions. It had to nag Majors like a dull headache that he might never break Coach Joe Paterno's iron grip on Eastern football.

It was Pitt's first victory over the Lions since 1965, Majors' first after his three straight assaults on the Lions had failed, 35-13, 31-10 and last year, 7-6. The victory, before 50,360 fans at Three Rivers Stadium and before a national television audience, solidifies the Panthers' No. 1 ranking and gives them their finest record ever, 11-0, to take against Georgia in the Sugar Bowl on New Year's Day.

Rumors are strong that Majors is planning to return to his alma mater, the University of Tennessee, as its new head coach. If he goes, it will be with the warm satisfaction of knowing he could climb that last Eastern mountain. If he stays, it will be with the knowledge that he has.

Pitt spotted the Lions' a 7-0 lead in the first quarter, caught them by halftime, then erupted out of a nifty little offensive wrinkle for 17 points in the second half.

It was not the man with the golden arm, quarterback Matt Cavanaugh, or the man with the golden legs, Dorsett, but the man with the broken jaw who made the difference.

Majors said he, like Paterno, had prepared some wrinkles during their two-week layoff, but said he wouldn't go to them unless he had to. He had to.

Joe Stone, a 6-4, 260-pound senior offensive tackle, who's been a second-stringer since a thug in Oakland broke his jaw with a bottle the night after the opening victory over Notre

---

In a surprise move, Tony Dorsett moved to fullback and rushed for 224 yards.

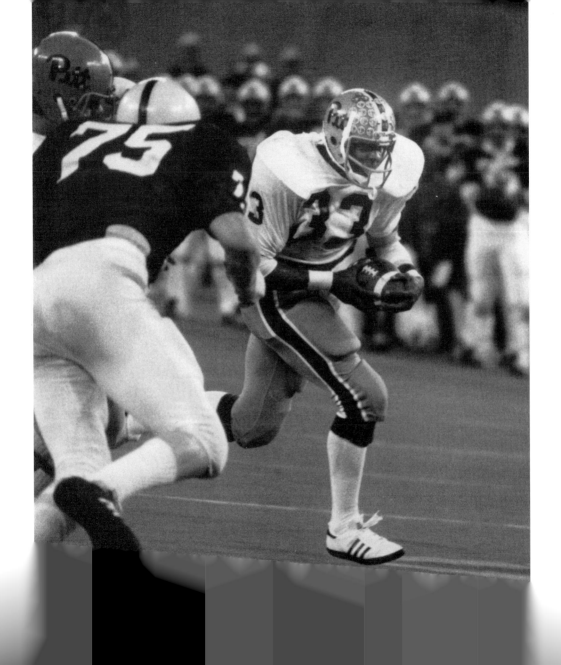

Dame, came in on an unbalanced line.

Dorsett, the tailback when Pitt goes to the "I" formation, moved to the up-back spot for some of the plays. Stone's position and play ruined Penn State's defensive work, and Dorsett, ripping off big chunks of yardage — his longest run was 42 yards — ruined what was left.

"Dorsett is some kind of back," Paterno said, a man who has praised the all-America for four years.

Fullback Bob Torrey gave Penn State its only touchdown on a 21-yard pass from quarterback Chuck Fusina with 3:01 left to play in the first quarter.

Dorsett (with Carson Long adding the extra point) got the score tied at 7-7 on a 6-yard run with 9:54 left in the first half. Dorsett then ripped 40 yards for another touchdown in the third quarter, halfback Elliott Walker slammed 12 yards for another in the fourth, and Long, redeeming his game-losing miss of last year, kicked a 47-yard field goal to wrap up the scoring.

Dorsett shook off a minor injury midway in the fourth quarter and came back to the game to push his record, as he had hoped, so far out of sight nobody would ever touch it.

His 224 yards gave him 6,082 career rushing yards. Nobody had ever rushed for 6,000 yards in college ball.

Bob Jury, the country's leader in pass interceptions, celebrates another steal.

Pitt Wins PSU's Favorite Trophy

By The Associated Press
Pittsburgh Post-Gazette

New York, Dec. 5, 1976 — Johnny Majors accepted the Lambert Trophy for the University of Pittsburgh's Eastern football champions yesterday and said he is glad Tennessee, his new team, doesn't have to face Pitt next year.

"There's no doubt in my mind that Pitt will be back here in the future, and I hope we play them in a bowl game some year," Majors said, "but I'm glad we don't have to play them next year."

Accepting the Lambert Trophy was one of Majors' last official acts before beginning preparations for top-ranked Pitt's Jan. 1 Sugar Bowl date with No. 5 Georgia.

At the same time, Coach Tubby Raymond of Delaware accepted the Lambert Cup for supremacy among middle-sized colleges in the East while Dom Anile of C.W. Post received the Lambert Bowl for the mythical Eastern small college crown.

In capturing the Lambert Trophy for the first time in 21 years, unbeaten Pitt ended Penn State's string of five consecutive Lamberts. Majors said he "saw the Lambert Trophy in the papers many times, but every time I saw it

(Penn State coach) Joe Paterno was holding it.

"Winning the Lambert Trophy was not because of Johnny Majors' coaching but because the Pitt administration made a commitment four years ago to be No. 1 in the East and No. 1 in the country."

With Jackie Sherrill, his successor as Pitt coach and his former chief aide, sitting alongside him, Majors said he was turning over "a good program."

Among the guests was Marshall Goldberg, a member of the team that won the first two Lambert Trophies in 1936-37 and holder of Pitt's career rushing record before Tony Dorsett broke it as a sophomore two years ago. Goldberg was an all-America in 1937-38.

"I was drafted by the Chicago Cardinals, I played 10 years with them and I've lived in Chicago ever since," Goldberg said, "so you can imagine how much I hate the Big Ten. All you hear is Big Ten this and Big Ten that. Now that Pitt's No. 1, I can finally open my mouth out there in Chicago.

"I remember when we got the Lambert Trophy the first year and again the second year. I thought it was ours for good."

Pitt's only other Eastern championship beside the first two years came in 1955.

He also set a single-season record of 1,948 topping Ed Marinaro's old record of 1,881, and set or tied a handful of other NCAA marks.

Like a kid shaping clay uncertainly, Pitt didn't begin to form its game until late in the first half. They struggled with poor field position, going deeper and deeper into the hole on punting exchanges. Six times they started inside their own 18, three times inside their own 8.

While the defense continued to snuff the Lions, confidence began to grow.

"Penn State fought us a helluva ball game," Majors said. "They were the aggressor in the first half. I don't think we had a second-and-short yardage play the whole first half, but the character of this team surfaced and would not be denied."

The break started to come when, with Dorsett like a man trapped in a phone booth, Cavanaugh began hurling lances to receiver Gordon Jones. Jones, limited for much of the season by injuries, had his best game, taking four passes for 111 yards. Cavanaugh, cool under the Lions' storied rush, hit eight of 16 and was intercepted twice.

The Lions' focus, a pinpoint on Dorsett, now had to expand to the entire field, and the Lions began to break down.

They dropped their first game after six straight victories and now will take a 7-4 record to the Gator Bowl against Notre Dame. It was

the end of a typical Paterno miracle. Penn State had lost three straight after an opening game victory and seemed doomed to their first losing season in, oh, a century or so.

Paterno made a daring and ingenious move by pulling his freshman linebackers, Bruce Clarke and Matt Millen, and inserting veterans Joe Diange and Tom DePaso in their places. He apparently felt the newcomers, although talented, were too much of a risk under the circumstances. It worked — until Majors upset the balance with his unbalanced line.

Randy Holloway (70) throws Lions quarterback Chuck Fusina for an 8-yard loss.

Pitt's defense was a choker. The Lions were held to 106 yards rushing, with a fleet of runners carrying 41 times. The passing game, aside from the touchdown strike, fell into disaster.

Pitt's Security Blanket defensive backfield — not a senior on it — allowed the Lions 135 yards and picked off four passes, a performance matching season highs against Notre Dame and Miami.

Junior Bob Jury took two to set a Pitt record of nine in a season. Jeff Delaney got one, his seventh, and J.C. Wilson got one, his second.

After the game, the ground crew spread the tarpaulin on the field. During the game, it seemed, Pitt had spread a net.

After a while, there was nowhere to turn — not on offense and not on defense.

The Lions mounted some fitted efforts in the third quarter, led principally by sophomore halfback Scott Fitzkee, whose touchdown led to Pitt's downfall last year. His 60 yards in 13 carries topped the Lions.

In the fourth, the Lions behaved strangely. With the score up to 24-7 and some seven minutes to play, they were sticking to the ground, as though trying to prove that they could get there without flying.

The end was apparent when Pitt muffled a big chance. Driving in the third quarter, they reached the Lions' 15 and fullback Bobby Hutton fumbled. Penn State's Joe Diminick recovered.

But the Lions were soon punting, on third down, seeking an abrupt escape.

Pitt got the ball at the 50. Dorsett over right guard for 7 yards, Dorsett around right end for 3 — and Dorsett, with a withering blast of speed, up the middle for 40 and a touchdown.

That was for 14-7, but it was the end.

SCORE BY PERIODS

Pitt	0	7	7	10	–	24
Penn State	7	0	0	0	–	7

Carson Long, redeemed after a game-losing miss in 1975, dances after his fourth-quarter goal.

Beating Lions Dorsett's Dessert

By Bob Black
The Pittsburg Press

Most people would be content with smashing every major college rushing record and being the primary Heisman Trophy candidate — despite anything you may have heard from out Southern California way.

Tony Dorsett, however, is not most people. For three years and going into the final game of this season, No. 33 — the guy who wore the only Pitt uniform ever to be retired — had already outdone such fast company as Archie Griffin and Ed Marinaro.

Last night, during Pitt's first victory over Penn State in 11 years, Dorsett added another two NCAA records to the nine he had previously held and tied four others while rushing for 224 yards on 38 carries.

Considering that four years ago Dorsett was merely the most highly sought high school product ever, who had narrowed his final choices down to Pitt and Penn State, last night's victory over the Nittany Lions capped everything else that might have mattered.

"It came down to a choice of where I might get the best opportunity," Dorsett said. "The chances of playing at Penn State right away weren't as good as they were at Pitt."

Had Dorsett gone to Penn State instead of Pitt, it might have been the Nittany Lions and not the Panthers who were the country's elite college football team this season.

It might also have meant that Dorsett wouldn't have had an opportunity to play four full seasons and become the leading college football rusher in history — gaining 6,082 yards on 1,074 carries — thus being the most obvious Heisman candidate Pitt has ever had.

But after three years of coming away frustrated by Penn State, Dorsett was still convinced he made the right choice four years ago.

"Tonight made it all worthwhile," he said, flashing a grin as quickly as he might have juked a linebacker on one of his long distance runs. "To tell you the truth, I never even thought about the Heisman when I went out there tonight. The only thing on my mind was beating Penn State.

"I realize there are other people on this team who have played against Penn State four years, but there's no way any of them can feel any better about this win than I do."

One of the guys who put in four years against Penn State along with Dorsett, also had attended Hopewell High School with him.

Ed Wilamowski, Pitt's defensive end who only saw limited action last night after suffering a pulled groin from the West Virginia game, has been Dorsett's teammate since eighth grade.

"He's the greatest athlete I've ever seen," Wilamowski said. "If he doesn't win the Heisman Trophy, then there's no justice. Having only lived a couple of miles away from him most of my life, I know how intense he is about football. There's probably not a harder worker around."

Another guy who has been with Dorsett for

"I never thought about the Heisman when I went out there. The only thing on my mind was beating Penn State."

four years — Coach Johnny Majors — was another person who couldn't begin to describe No. 33's worth.

"He's the greatest practice player I've ever had," Majors said. "He's all seriousness out there. That's what makes him such a great football player."

As far as Majors was concerned, "beating Penn State was the biggest thrill of my life to date, but Tony Dorsett has given me more than enough thrills to last me a long time.

"I realize it was our entire team that won it," Majors said, "but right now there just aren't words to express how I feel about Tony Dorsett."

Regarding all the talk that without Dorsett and Majors, the Panther football fortunes would still be down where they were four years ago, No. 33 disagrees.

"No one person turns around a football program," Dorsett said. "I've never seen one man be an entire football team — no way. It took us four years to do something like this and I'm just glad to be a part of it."

"Although Tony was the man people came to see," Majors said. "I have to agree that it was the team effort which did it."

The little things — like usual monster man Dave DiCiccio taking just a week and a half to learn a new position and filling in admirably for Wilamowski — and Bob Jury setting a team record for interceptions (nine) in a season — and injured Elliott Walker crashing the final 12 yards for a touchdown — and place-kicker Carson Long finally getting rid of the hex he's had against Penn State with a 47-yard field goal were all a part of it.

But mostly, it was No. 33, saving one of his most impressive performances for Pitt's biggest victory in a decade.

Anybody watching Dorsett had to be impressed.

Come Tuesday, when they announce the Heisman Trophy winner, No. 33 should get his due reward.

91

Dorsett Wins Heisman Trophy

By United Press International
The Pittsburgh Press

New York, Nov. 30, 1976 — Tony Dorsett of Pittsburgh, the 1976 rushing champion and the only player ever to gain more than 6,000 yards in a career, today was named winner of the Heisman Trophy as the outstanding college football player in the nation.

Ricky Bell of Southern California, runnerup in last year's voting, finished second again and Rob Lytle of Michigan was third.

As expected, the balloting wasn't close as Dorsett won by 1,011 points. The 5-foot-11, 196 pound senior from Aliquippa, Pa., collected 701 first-place votes and 2,357 points from the 863 sportswriters and sportscasters from across the nation who participated in the voting.

Bell had 73 first-place votes and 1,346 points while Lytle was named first on 35 ballots and had 413 points.

Dorsett is the first Pitt player ever to win the Heisman Trophy and only the second eastern

The Ballot

The tabulation of votes from 863 registered and qualified electors from coast to coast for this year, 1976, is as follows:

Total Points

1. Tony Dorsett, Pittsburgh	2,357
2. Ricky Bell, So. California	1,346
3. Rob Lytle, Michigan	413
4. Terry Miller, Oklahoma St.	197
5. Tommy Kramer, Rice	63
6. Gifford Nielsen, Brigham Young	45
7. Ray Goff, Georgia	44
8. Mike Voight, No. Carolina	41
9. Joe Roth, California	32
10. Jeff Dankworth, UCLA	31

player to be so honored in the last 13 years. John Cappellitti of Penn State, now a running back with the Los Angeles Rams, won the Heisman Trophy in 1973.

After finishing a "shocking" fourth last year

Tony Dorsett was the first Pitt player to win the Heisman Trophy.

THE HEISMAN MEMORIAL TROPHY
AWARDED ANNUALLY TO THE OUTSTANDING COLLEGE FOOTBALL PLAYER IN THE
UNITED STATES BY THE DOWNTOWN ATHLETIC CLUB OF NEW YORK CITY, INC.
WINNERS TO DATE

1964 - JOHN HUARTE,
UNIVERSITY OF NOTRE DAME
1965 - MICHAEL GARRETT,
UNIVERSITY OF SOUTHERN CALIFORNIA
1966 - STEPHEN SPURRIER, UNIVERSITY OF FLORIDA
1967 - GARY BERAN, UNIVERSITY OF CALIFORNIA,
LOS ANGELES
1968 - O.J. SIMPSON,
UNIVERSITY OF SOUTHERN CALIFORNIA
1969 - STEVE OWENS, UNIVERSITY OF OKLAHOMA
1970 - JIM PLUNKETT, STANFORD UNIVERSITY

1971 - PAT SULLIVAN, AUBURN UNIVERSITY
1972 - JOHNNY RODGERS, NEBRASKA UNIVERSITY
1973 - JOHN CAPPELLETTI, PENNSYLVANIA STATE UNIVERSITY
1974 - ARCHIE M. GRIFFIN, OHIO STATE UNIVERSITY
1975 - ARCHIE M. GRIFFIN, OHIO STATE UNIVERSITY

when Ohio State's Archie Griffin became the first player ever to win the Heisman twice, Dorsett set his sights on winning the award this season. He began on a strong note by rushing for 181 yards and a touchdown in a victory over Notre Dame and rushed for over 200 yards in a game four times during the season as Pittsburgh went unbeaten and earned the No. 1 ranking in the nation.

During his four-year career, Dorsett established 13 NCAA rushing records, including most career yardage (6,082). He gained 1,948 yards this season for an average of 177 yards per game and scored 22 touchdowns.

Bell, the nation's leading rusher a year ago, was expected to challenge Dorsett for the Heisman but the 6-2, 225-pound senior tailback was injured for part of the year and gained 675 yards less than last season.

Bell did have the nation's best single-game rushing performance this season (347 yards against Washington State), but he was hobbled by injuries over the last six games of the year and surpassed the 100-yard barrier only once during that span.

Dorsett was the top vote-getter in every section of the country, with Bell second in all five sections.

Terry Miller, a junior running back from Oklahoma State, was fourth with 197 points, followed in order by quarterback Tommy Kramer of Rice, quarterback Gifford Nielsen of

Dorsett's Records

Tony Dorsett rushed for 224 yards on 38 carries, giving him a career total of 6,082 yards on 1,074 carries. Dorsett now has 13 major college marks. Listed below are the most significant:

• Most Yards Gained — Season: 1,948 (surpassing Ed Marinaro's 1971 record of 1,881)
• Most Games Gaining 100 Yards or More: 11 (season record, tying Griffin), 33 (career mark, also tying Griffin)
• Most Touchdowns Scored — Career: 59 (tying Glenn Davis of Army, 1943-46)
• Most Points Scored — Career: 356 (surpassing Davis' record of 354)

Brigham Young, quarterback Ray Goff of Georgia, running back Mike Voight of North Carolina, quarterback Joe Roth of California and quarterback Jeff Dankworth of UCLA.

Others receiving votes were quarterback Vince Ferragamo of Nebraska, wide receiver Larry Sievers of Tennessee, fullback Pete Johnson of Ohio State and quarterback Rick Leach of Michigan.

Tony D: 11-0 Tells It All

By Phil Axelrod
Special to The Post-Gazette

Pittsburgh, Nov. 27, 1976 — Leave it to the man who tarnished Notre Dame's Golden Dome to exorcise Penn State and Joe Paterno's jinx over Pitt's Panthers.

Tony Dorsett, who has accomplished more than any other player in the history of college football, did what long-suffering Pitt fans have waited 10 years for someone to do ... beat Penn State.

Doing it with his customary flair and feel for the dramatic, Dorsett slashed, pounded and skittered his way for 224 yards and two touchdowns to lead the Panthers to a 24-7 victory over Penn State at Three Rivers Stadium last night.

"Being 11-0 means more than anything to me," Dorsett told a pack of reporters crowded into Pitt's steaming locker room. "It means a lot to us to beat Joe Paterno."

Pausing to catch his breath as reporters fired questions in rapid succession, Dorsett added, "We were No. 1 going into the game, and we're No. 1 coming out of it."

However, during a tense first half, Dorsett and Pitt's 33-points-a-game offense were being stymied by Penn State's swarming defense.

"At times," said Dorsett, "I was wondering what was going on. Penn State always gives us a new look they haven't shown all season. It took us a while to pick it up."

But for half a game, at least, Dorsett was stopped. Cold.

"It was like ice out there," Dorsett said of the Tartan Turf that soaked up a steady rain all night. "For a while, I didn't think I'd get untracked."

Once Dorsett found the right track, he kept going ... and going ... and going. The second half was all Dorsett.

"Any great back gets stronger as the game goes on," said Dorsett, who gained 173 of those yards after the intermission.

Dorsett picked up many of those yards as Johnny Majors put a new little wrinkle in the Pitt "I" formation. Dorsett, normally the deep back, was moved up a step or two as the up-back.

"It let me read the blocks faster," Dorsett said.

When asked if he was getting tired lugging the ball 38 times, Dorsett raised his eyebrows, cocked his head back and smiled. "I've waited four years for this, so I wasn't going to let myself get tired," he said.

Dorsett: Definitely a Nuclear Weapon

By Shelly Anderson

It's not something Tony Dorsett pops into the VCR very often, but in the summer of 1996 a buddy visiting the former football star bugged him to watch the 1976 Pitt highlight film.

What the heck.

Music that is pure 1970's — did we really listen to all that tinny, whiny disco? — accompanies images that are a bit rough around the edges, thanks to the film-to-video process. After running through about half the season, the tape segues off into a tribute to Dorsett. The music is different now, the classic "My Way" sung by Frank Sinatra. There is Tony, 20 years younger, No. 33 in the white road jersey, gliding in slow motion, sloughing off Navy defensive players on his way to the end zone.

When Dorsett pulls up after a 32-yard touchdown run, he is mobbed by his teammates. He falls to the bottom of the pile, is pulled up, yanked this way and that. It is a moment of sheer triumph. Dorsett has just broken Archie Griffin's record to become the top career rusher in college football.

"Every time I watch that, it brings tears to my eyes, even after 20 years," Dorsett said.

And that moment was just a slice of one of the greatest seasons a college running back has clocked in and out of. Dorsett won the Heisman Trophy, became a four-time all-American and four-time 1,000-yard rusher and carried Pitt to an undefeated season and a national championship.

It had started building in 1973, when Dorsett was the centerpiece of a recruiting class brought in by new Pitt coach Johnny Majors that various people remember as being anywhere from 65 to 100 strong.

A star for Hopewell High in neighboring Beaver County, Dorsett had decided to stay close to home and chase a chance to play immediately. He opened his college career with a 100-yard day in a tie at Georgia and went on to an all-American season of 1,586 yards rushing and 12 touchdowns for the most improved NCAA team of 1973 — from 1-10 to 6-5-1, including the

"He had great eyes — great, big eyes," Majors said. "He saw everything on the field."

Panthers' first bowl trip in 17 years.

By the time he was finished at Pitt, Dorsett had logged 6,082 yards rushing (6,626 including bowl games), had set or tied 18 college rushing records and was being called the best college back in history.

It didn't slow down following 1976.

After Dorsett's college career, which landed him a spot in the College Football Hall of Fame, he was the Dallas Cowboys' first-round pick in the NFL draft and earned a Super Bowl championship ring as a rookie. He played 13 years in the NFL, rushing for 12,739 yards and making it a distinctive double by being elected to the Pro Football Hall of Fame.

But in 1976, Tony (T.D.) Dorsett played the game better than anyone.

"He was definitely a nuclear weapon," said John Pelusi, the center on that veteran team, one of several recruits who came in with Majors in 1973.

"With someone like him, you went into the game with a lot of confidence," said Tom Brzoza, a junior guard in '76. "He didn't need much room. All he needed was a crack."

Majors believes Dorsett — who brought with him to Pitt 4.3-second speed in the 40-yard dash and the childhood nickname of "Hawk" — had not only ability but also great instinct and vision.

"He had great eyes — great, big eyes," Majors said. "He saw everything on the field."

Majors had such respect for Dorsett that he purposely limited the coaching he aimed at his star running back. It amounted to showing Dorsett the alignments and plays, pointing out the tendencies of the upcoming opponent's defense during meetings and film sessions, then sitting back to watch.

It wasn't that Majors didn't know how to handle such a talent. Quite the opposite.

"I've seen some people baby a great player too much and just almost become subservient to the player," Majors said. "On the other hand, I've seen many coaches smother a good player, try to coach him all the time when you really should spend more time coaching the other ones. Tony was the kind of person you didn't need to smother. Once you showed him what you wanted, you didn't have to tell him again. He did that thing to perfection and did it with great effort. Why should I spoil it for Tony Dorsett, telling him something on every play or even every day?"

Majors recalls just one instance when he offered Dorsett advice. As an all-American tailback and Heisman Trophy runner-up in Tennessee's single-wing offense of the mid-1950's,

---

In 4 seasons, Dorsett and Johnny Majors turned lowly Pitt into national champions.

Majors gained great insight to several aspects of the game.

During Dorsett's sophomore year, the coach spotted a tic in his game that looked familiar. Dorsett, Majors said, was overusing his natural ability to stop and start, to make a little head fake and then fly.

He called Dorsett to his office.

"I said, 'Tony, there's something I notice you're doing.' I said, 'My junior year, the line coach noticed that I was making one or two movements too much. I didn't even realize it. But what we told me helped because it took the lost motion out. There's no reason for it. If I make one move, I'm gone. If I make two, I'll possibly run right back into [the defensive player].' I told him, 'That's a personal experience. So take a look at the films.' And he did do that."

By the time 1976 rolled around, there was no hitch in Dorsett's get-along.

The season began with a great challenge for him. As a junior Dorsett had embarrassed Notre Dame with 303 yards rushing on 23 carries as Pitt beat the Fighting Irish for the first time in a decade. For 1976, ABC television, smelling a great national matchup, maneuvered to move the Pitt-Notre Dame game to the front of the season.

The Irish hadn't forgotten — or forgiven —

Dorsett. All through spring drills, the players said they were masterminding great plans to stop the pesky Pitt runner. The sentiment only grew leading up to the game.

Dorsett remembers stuffed No. 33's hanging in effigy from windows all over the Notre Dame campus, and mock tombstones bearing his name. The Panthers swear the Irish grew the grass on their field to 3 inches to slow Dorsett. "You could not see your shoes," Pelusi said.

Pitt was undaunted.

"There was no intimidation factor going in there," Brzoza said. "Everybody talks about the aura of playing Notre Dame. It seems like we were over that hump. We beat them the year before and Tony ran crazy on them."

On the game's first possession, Notre Dame ate up several minutes and drove for a touchdown and a 7-0 lead. "The crowd was beyond themselves, wild," Majors said. "They kicked it off. Out of bounds. And they're still wild."

Tackle Joe Stone jumped offside before the Panthers' first snap, and Pitt had a first-and-15 at its 15. Majors, telling his staff it was too early to panic, ordered a simple counter dive — base blocking, Dorsett gets the ball. He cracked through the backfield, bounced outside at the line and ran 61 yards. Five plays later, he ran wide for a touchdown to tie the game. "The

100

President Gerald Ford visits with Dorsett after the Navy game in 1976.

When the circus came to town, Dorsett was asked to lead the parade.

silence that overcame that crowd was something," Dorsett said.

He finished with 181 yards and Pitt won, 31-10.

"He always played well," Majors said, "but he was best in the tougher situations. And the more he carried the ball, the better he got during the course of the game."

The Panthers began flying through the schedule, beating Georgia Tech, Temple, Duke, Louisville and Miami, with Dorsett piling up the yards. Going into the seventh game, at Navy, Dorsett needed 152 yards to break Griffin's all-time rushing record. The next week, Pitt would be at home against Syracuse, so Dorsett had mixed emotions.

"Something like that, you like to do it in your own back yard," he said. "But it's the nature of sports — if you've got something going, go for it." The Panthers, on the Navy 32 in the fourth quarter, were comfortably ahead (they won, 45-0) and Dorsett was 4 yards shy of the mark. Majors considered yanking the first team, but Pelusi talked him into giving it one shot.

That was all Dorsett needed. When he crossed the goal line, the first of his teammates to surround him were the linemen. "We knew he was going to set it, so we didn't block anybody," Brzoza said. "We just ran down to meet him." The celebration even included the hosts. Navy shot off its cannon — something normally reserved for hometeam accomplishments —

and its corps gave Dorsett a salute.

A few days later, Dorsett met the Commander in Chief, Gerald Ford, who was traveling through Pittsburgh and arranged to meet with the player and Majors at the airport. Dorsett gave President Ford a blue and gold button, "Pitt's No. 1," and later said he was "really surprised that the president knew me."

Didn't know him? Judging from the requests for his time and the attention he drew from various media, you would have had to look under some pretty big rocks to find anyone in the country who hadn't heard of Tony Dorsett.

Dorsett, quiet but not to the point of reticence, obliged as best he could. "I'm always one of the last guys out of the locker room," Majors said, "and I can see him after a game, to this day, after carrying the ball 20, 30, 35 times, pretty tired and sore, outside the locker room signing autographs for those kids. He had a natural knack for dealing with people."

He just didn't have a lot of spare time.

"Everyone wanted to come in and do feature stories," said Dean Billick, the Pitt sports information director at the time. "The difficulty I had was making sure Tony had enough time to be a student and be a football player and try to have a little bit of time for himself. We even had to set up a specific time once a week and have him sit down with groups for interviews."

At one point late in the season, Phyllis George came to Pittsburgh and got a one-on-

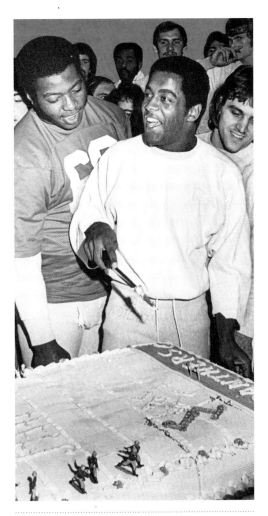

Dorsett and his teammates celebrate his NCAA rushing record.

one for CBS. As she strolled with Dorsett through the campus, he surprised everyone by telling her his name was dor-SETT, not DOR-sett. "I got my scoop!" George later told Billick.

In the Panthers' final game at Pitt Stadium, against backyard rival West Virginia, the school retired No. 33 at halftime, the first jersey to be so honored. Athletic Director Cas Myslinski made the announcement at midfield. Majors, grinning broadly, shook Dorsett's hand, then wrapped his arm around Dorsett's neck. Dorsett, smiling but almost a little sheepish, unfolded a jersey identical to the one he was wearing and held it up to the cheering crowd.

Dorsett would have picked up his fifth 200-yard game of the season that day except that, at 199, he got ejected when he came up swinging on a late hit near the Pitt bench.

In the Panthers' regular-season finale, it was Penn State that got cold-cocked. The game had been moved to a Friday night at Three Rivers Stadium, and the Nittany Lions had won 10 straight in the series. It was tied, 7-7, at halftime, thanks in part to an effective Penn State defense that did a lot of moving and shifting.

Majors crossed up that defense. He went with an unbalanced line for the first time since he had been at Pitt and lined up Dorsett in the fullback spot of the I-formation. "It was just a little wrinkle," Dorsett said. "They threw me in that I-formation and, bam!, hit that seam and go." He finished the game with 224 yards and two TD's to go over 6,000 yards for his career, and Pitt won, 24-7.

Next up for Pitt was the Sugar Bowl, but there was a pit stop in New York for Dorsett, to accept the Heisman Trophy. He won in a landslide, earning 701 of the 842 first-place votes.

In New Orleans, the Panthers had only to beat Georgia to secure the national championship. Majors, Dorsett and the rest of that recruiting class remembered the Bulldogs from that '73 opener. Pitt had taken the field in Athens under a hail of abuse from the fans. "Dog meat!" they had screamed — and Dorsett later admitted he was a bit frightened and unsure — but a 7-7 final shut them up.

Then, a tie was the equivalent of a tremendous upset. This time, only a win would do. With Keith Jackson and Ara Parseghian describing it for ABC, Dorsett set a Sugar Bowl record with 202 yards and Pitt won, 27-3.

"Our class started against Georgia, and we ended against them," Dorsett said. "That was kind of nice." A bookend finish to a story-book season and college career for T.D.

After his graduation, Dorsett's locker became a Pitt shrine.

How Sweet It Is!

By Russ Franke
Special to The Pittsburgh Press

New Orleans — Johnny Majors didn't have to stick his finger in the air to signify his Pitt team was No. 1 in the nation yesterday. His team stuck its offense and defense right up where a national television audience and a Superdome full of people could see what a champion is made of.

The Panthers completely dominated Georgia's fourth-ranked Bulldogs in the Sugar Bowl, 27-3, to give Pitt its first national championship in 39 years in a game that was supposed to be an even match. They also gave Majors and most of his staff a super going-away present in his last game as Pitt coach.

The national title climaxed a four-year job at Pitt for Majors, who will officially become the Tennessee coach when he signs a long-term contract to return to his old school.

It turned out, as insiders expected all along, that his announced departure had no effect whatever on the morale of the Pitt team, which has put together possibly its best all-around

game of a 12-0 season, Pitt's best ever.

It was the first time a team from the East won the Sugar Bowl since Navy did it in 1955 and only the third win for an Eastern team in 43 games here.

The Pitt defense completely out-classed Georgia's Junkyard Dogs with a glowing reputation for chasing the ball, gang-tackling and terrorizing the rest of the teams in the Southeastern Conference. The Panthers stole the show early by forcing Georgia into passing situations and picked off four interceptions in the first half. By intermission the score was 21-0 and the Bulldog fans in the crowd of 76,117 became noticeably quieter.

Offensively, Matt Cavanaugh took care of the passing and Tony Dorsett was his sensational self in rushing for 202 yards on 32 carries, breaking a 32-year old Sugar Bowl record as a wind-

Johnny Majors celebrates Pitt's win. It would be his final game as the Panthers' coach.

up to the most brilliant career of any rusher in college history. Cavanaugh won the game's MVP award, completing 10 of 18 passes for 192 yards.

Georgia didn't sustain a drive all day and was fortunate to escape a shutout on Allan Leavitt's 25-yard field goal set up by a Pitt fumble.

Pitt's scores came on a 6-yard run by Cavanaugh, a 59-yard pass from Cavanaugh to Gordon Jones, an 11-yard sweep by Dorsett and field goals of 42 and 31 yards by Carson Long, the most productive kick-scorer in NCAA history. They were the highlights of 480 yards in total offense, and as someone in the press box observed, "Pitt made the Junkyard Dogs look more like Hot Dogs."

His remark was kind compared to what Georgia people were saying about Pitt all week. The Pitt team shared the hotel with droves of Georgians who heckled and insulted the Panthers at every opportunity.

There was also a great deal of unfavorable comment in the local paper about Majors' lax policy with his team — imposing no curfew until two nights before the game. The Southerners strongly disapproved of reports of Pitt players carousing on Bourbon Street until the late hours.

The Pitt team took it all in stride until game-

Final AP Top 20

Team	Record	Pts.
1. Pitt (59)	12-0-0	1,234
2. Southern Cal (3)	11-1-0	1,118
3. Michigan	10-2-0	847
4. Houston	10-2-0	804
5. Oklahoma	9-2-1	638
6. Ohio State	9-2-1	510
7. Texas A&M	10-2-0	487
8. Maryland	11-1-0	445
9. Nebraska	9-3-1	422
10. Georgia	10-2-0	388
11. Alabama	9-3-0	331
12. Notre Dame	9-3-0	321
13. Texas Tech	10-2-0	276
14. Oklahoma State	9-3-0	190
15. UCLA	9-2-1	172
16. Colorado	8-4-0	52
17. Rutgers	11-0-0	50
18. Kentucky	8-4-0	30
19. Iowa State	8-3-0	14
20. Mississippi State	9-2-0	11

time, attacking the Bulldogs with grim emotion. "We didn't go somewhere else (the Orange Bowl and a million dollars)," said Majors. "We came here so we could play for the national

---

Tony Dorsett rushed for 202 yards and 1 TD against Georgia.

championship. After the game I told our team that I could never hope to relive another four years like the past four."

Asked whether he thought the outcome would convince the West Coast and the Michigan and Southern Cal coaches as to who is undoubtedly No. 1, Majors said, "I wasn't trying to convince anyone but Georgia."

Strategically, Pitt used the "I" formation more than in any previous game and got the most out of its passing in key situations.

The Panthers scored on their second possession with an 80-yard drive spurred by passes of 13 yards to Jones and 36 yards to Elliott Walker.

The pass to Walker on a flood pattern in the middle carried to the 10. Dorsett crashed for 4 yards and Cavanaugh stepped inside left tackle from the 6 for the score. A fourth-and-1 gamble at midfield paid off in keeping the drive going and setting the stage for a ball control game (the Panthers had the ball for 36 minutes to Georgia's 24).

Two more scores came in the second period after the Pitt defense had held Georgia inside its own territory and linebackers Arnie Weatherington and Jim Cramer intercepted passes.

Weatherington stole Ray Goff's pass at the Pitt 26 and the Cavanaugh-to-Jones combination struck suddenly after a 15-yard flat pass to flanker Willie Taylor on the Pitt 41. Cavanaugh found Jones in the middle and Jones broke a tackle and skipped all the way for a touchdown.

Georgia sent its passing quarterback, Matt Robinson, into the game and on Robinson's first series, Cramer, Weatherington's sidekick at linebacker picked off a throw on the Pitt 33. Cavanaugh passed 10 yards to tight end Jim Corbett and Dorsett made his first breakaway run of the day, 22 yards to the Bulldog 22. Taylor caught a pass for 14 yards and Dorsett swept around the right side 11 yards for a score.

Long's kick made it 21-0 with two minutes to play and with Georgia trying to score a quick one. Leroy Felder and Bob Jury both made interceptions, the 27th and 28th of the season by Pitt.

A few minutes into the third period, Georgia got its first break when Walker dropped a handoff and Georgia's Lawrence Craft recovered on the Pitt 25. The Pitt defense, notably tackle Randy Holloway, gave up only two yards on three plays, forcing Leavitt's field goal.

Dorsett was just getting warmed up, after gaining 65 yards in the first half. He blazed through the middle on a sprint draw 67 yards

Matt Cavanaugh (12) scored Pitt's first TD after faking to Dorsett.

to the 18 and only a diving tackle by corner-back Johnny Henderson saved a touchdown. The Junkyard Dogs finally got tough and shoved Pitt back to the 25, and Long came in to boot his 42-yard field goal to make it 24-3.

Al Chesley, taking over at linebacker after Cramer injured his ankle, recovered Goff's fumble on the Georgia 23 to set up Long's 31-yard field goal. Toward the end, with reserves on the field and Tom Yewcic quarterbacking, the clock killed Pitt's last chance for another touchdown with the ball on the 8.

Al Romano, Pitt's all-American middle guard, said he wasn't surprised that Pitt dominated the game defensively. "All your people didn't give our defense enough credit — all they knew was Tony Dorsett and the offense. Georgia wasn't prepared for the way we chased the ball. We have one of the best defenses in the country — our linebackers were super today and we did a good job of stopping Goff's runs."

Monster Jeff Delaney said the Panthers wanted a shutout after the first quarter. "It was our best game, on the whole, for us all year," he said.

SCORE BY PERIODS

Pittsburgh	7	14	3	3	–	27
Georgia	0	0	3	0	–	3

Cavanaugh, with the game's MVP trophy, greets Pitt fans at the Pittsburgh Airport.

Party Line: One Champ, It's Pitt

By Marino Parascenzo
Special to The Post-Gazette

They gave a No. 1 party, and no one came. Not Woody, not Bo, and not John. Some said not Georgia and its Junkyard Dogs, either. And wouldn't you know it? — no champagne, either.

Not much of a party spirit, for that matter. The Pitt Panthers trotted back to their dressing room, to nothing wetter than a hot shower, wearing so-whats on their faces. Could this be the football team that had just won the national championship?

Well, it truly was all over, but the election. The landslide had already taken place. Georgia's Bulldogs had just been buried on the Superdome turf, 27-3, in the 1977 Sugar Bowl. It hardly mattered that on a crisp Saturday New Year's afternoon, the Orange and Rose Bowls still had to be played.

Woody Hayes of Ohio State, angry at something, deduced that Pitt chose the Sugar in order to avoid playing the Colorado team he would meet. And in Pasadena, Bo Schembechler of Michigan and John Robinson of Southern Cal proclaimed that their Rose Bowl game would decide the national title, no matter what the rest of the country said.

Al Romano, the Pitt middle guard, had his solution, "Did the Rose Bowl start yet?" he said, bending to cut the tape from his ankles. "No? Well, go tell them to call it off. Tell them not to bother."

Pitt entered the Sugar Bowl No. 1 in both wire service polls. And when you've stepped out of the Sugar Bowl like a puppy coming out of a card house, and you've left No. 5 Georgia 10-2, and gasping in their own wreckage, why, all you need then is for the National Broadcasting Company to anoint you.

The official word on the unofficial national championship should be forthcoming shortly from the wire services. Meanwhile, the question remains, which play worked best — Dorsett off tackle, Cavanaugh-to-whoever, or a sweep through the French Quarter?

They've quit telling ethnic jokes in New Orleans. Now it's Pitt jokes. "The Georgia players are now in bed," said one television guy on the 11 p.m. news, "and Pitt is just getting dressed to go out." "Majors posted a curfew," another gag went. "He told them to be in by February."

It all began when Southern media people went pale when they learned that Johnny Majors, author of Pitt's success and now officially the Tennessee coach, let his players maintain their on-campus lifestyle. Which meant no curfews until a couple of days before the game, and freedom to roam. At the same time, Georgia's players were being bed-checked at something like 10:30 p.m.

Contrary to popular belief, both Biloxi, Miss., site of the first week's drills, and the French Quarter were still there at last look.

The Panthers, at first surprised by the reaction, missed few chances to embellish the notion they were the big partying team out of the effete East.

Defensive tackle Don Parrish, for example, was limping toward the locker room on his sprained ankle. Someone wanted to know whether it was serious. "Oh, it will be all right," Parrish said, "soon as I have a couple of drinks."

After the game, a Georgia fan at the Pitt hotel headquarters, noting the Georgia curfew, lifted his hands and sighed, "So much for clean living."

The game was over quickly. Pitt struck for a 21-0 lead in the first half — quarterback Matt Cavanaugh trotting 6 yards for the first touchdown, hitting receiver Gordon Jones on a 59-yard pass play for the second score, and Tony Dorsett swishing 11 yards for the third. Then, aside from two field goals by Carson Long, Pitt

Dorsett joins the Pitt fans' post-game chanting of "We're No. 1."

sat on the second half.

"We wanted to eat up the clock," Majors said. Get it over with, he meant.

The Panthers had to survive not only the nightlife, but also a bout of virus that put down about eight players and four children accompanying the teams, as well as the boisterous nagging of Georgia fans.

A large contingent lodged at the Marriott where the Pitt team stayed. What started as good fun degenerated into harassment Pitt players found barely bearable. One night, a lobby mob refused to part and let Dorsett and tight end Jim Corbett reach the elevators.

At the Superdome, it was Pitt's turn. While Dorsett was rushing to a Sugar Bowl record of 202 yards and Cavanaugh was picking up the Most Valuable Player Award, the Pitt people joked.

The jokes were perfectly awful. "It's a dog's life." "Their bark is worse than their bite." "They're more bull than dog." Like that. But they had a kind of healing effect on the sores of that pre-game abuse.

What was happening was that Georgia's 1,000 yard rusher, Kevin McLee of Uniontown, Pa., was kept busy getting 48 yards in his 14 carries. And quarterback Ray Goff, the Southeastern Conference's player of the year, who had 724 for the year, got 76. Goff and three other Bulldogs quarterbacks got off a total of 22 passes. Three were completed to Georgia guys

and four to Pitt guys. Pitt also took in two fumbles, improving on its average of four turnovers per game.

The tale is complete in the Sugar Bowl's profit-and-loss statement. The Georgia offense had averaged 336 yards and 29 points per game. It got 181 and 3. The Junkyard dog defense had allowed averages of 271 yards and 10 points. It gave up 480 and 27.

One of the Georgia quarterbacks was Tony Flanagan, a 6-3 sophomore, who is also a standout on the Georgia basketball team. Dooley called on Flanagan midway through the fourth quarter to get something started. Anything. Flanagan dropped back to pass on his first play and was crushed for an 8-yard loss by Pitt defensive tackle Randy Holloway.

It was a clumsy social moment for Holloway. He and Flanagan had become friends playing together in an all-star basketball tournament in Sharon, Pa., some years earlier. What do you say to an old friend you just planted?

"Well, uh ... " Holloway paused, embarrassed. "I said, well, uh, 'Hello, Tony.' "

Flanagan wasn't invited to the post-game party. It wasn't a farewell party thrown by Majors, who left early yesterday for Hawaii and the Hula Bowl with Dorsett, Romano and Corbett. It was a welcome party thrown by Jackie Sherrill, the new Pitt coach. Well, at least he was off to the right start.

Majors: Pride, Energy and Enthusiasm

BY CHUCK FINDER

Pitt wasn't it for Johnny Majors at first. No big city was the place for him. Or so he thought in the fall of 1972. Back then, the telephone lines to Ames, Iowa, were jammed with suitors. Kentucky, Michigan State, Purdue all wooed the dashing, drawling Iowa State football coach. But no one was more persistent, no one a more regular caller than C.R. (Bob) Miller, a booster from Pitt.

Every Thursday night, when the Iowa State gameplan was done and the energetic coach was exhaling at long last, the desk phone would ring. Miller would spend the next hour or so chatting up the 37-year-young coach, trying to convince him to consider Pittsburgh. Majors would make polite conversation, thank him for calling and hang up wincing. Pittsburgh?

"I'm a small-town boy," explained John Terrill Majors of the Huntland, Tenn., Majorses. He was the eldest son of Shirley Majors, for 34 years a football coach in East Tennessee high schools and the University of Sewanee. He was the star, the 1956 Heisman Trophy runner-up, of a family of boys who draped themselves in Saturday afternoon glory: Bill and Bobby at the University of Tennessee like Johnny; Joe at Florida State; Larry at Sewanee with Coach Dad. He was a big man on campus after campus, working hard as an assistant coach at his alma mater in Knoxville, then at Mississippi State in Starkville and Arkansas in Fayetteville. In 1968, he went to Ames, Iowa, and took a starving Big Eight program to its first two bowls ever. Then Pitt called. And called. And called. Was it dialing up Arizona State's Frank Kush (from nearby Windber) or North Carolina's Homer Smith as often?

"But I didn't know if I even wanted to visit or not," Majors remembered. "'Cause I was getting other calls. And I didn't think I wanted to live in a city whatsoever."

Just to be sure, he dispatched his little brother Joe, a lawyer, on a fact-finding mission. Joe came to the city under an assumed name. He met with Pitt administrators as a representative

Johnny Majors left a booming Iowa State team to resurrect Pitt's football fortunes.

of an interested coach. Little brother then traveled to Ames to watch big brother's Iowa State team tie Nebraska. Afterward, he pulled aside his big brother and delivered this Pitt report: "It's the place for you. They're hungry to be competitive again. They're ready to move. And you're the man to show them how to do it."

Meanwhile, back in Pittsburgh, Pitt Chancellor Wesley Posvar caught a glimpse of this Johnny Majors fellow on the television news. He recognized the wide smile, the straight hair, the ears. "That guy I met wasn't Joe Mason, it was Joe Majors."

Decades later, Johnny Majors smiled that wide smile at the memory of it all. He relished the irony of the events that brought him to Pittsburgh and the mountaintop of college football. Turned out, this big city was the place for him.

The small-town boy became a small wonder in the Steel City. He fed its competitive hunger. He moved it to the forefront of a sport it owned on fall Fridays and Sundays, between its ballyhooed high schools and its professional Steelers. Johnny Majors transformed a 1-10 team into a 6-4-1 bowl invitee and became the Football Writers Association Division I coach of the year in his first season, 1973, at the same time Coach Dad was the writers' choice for Small College coach of the year. He became the Division I coach of the year again in 1976, when he steered Pitt to an 11-0 record and the national championship.

"Those days," says middle guard Al Romano, "it was magic."

"I mean, I was sitting in the locker room ... in what looks like a bomb shelter," Romano began, going back to the beginning — the recruiting winter of 1973.

"Cement floor, it's all wet. Old, beat-up steel lockers. Everything was rundown. I thought, 'Man, this guy's gotta be good.' When he was talking to me, I was looking for a door, to go look for somebody to hit. I thought, 'What's this guy, Houdini or something?' "

When Majors accepted Pitt's offer a week before Iowa State's 1972 Liberty Bowl date, so much was still vapor. There was no contract to sign for at least another two weeks. There wasn't but two assistants at the start. Just a few promises and a heap of plans. The day after Iowa State lost that game, Majors was announced to the Pittsburgh media, looking like a grinning Sherriff Andy from Mayberry seated between stoic West Pointers Posvar and Pitt Athletic Director Cas Myslinski. He promised to turn lemons into lemonade. Eight of his 11 Pitt assistants followed him east from Ames, and they quickly commenced to squeezing out a champion.

The new coach had been promised 50 scholarships each of the first four seasons of his five-year deal. The number was almost double what Carl DePasqua and staff had to offer previously, and the money was stowed in a booster account that probably would set off NCAA alarms were it years later. But the problem in the winter of 1973 was, Majors and his assistants were so dogged, so sleepless on the recruiting trail, they surpassed their allotment. By, oh, half.

Seventy-five players they brought in. Although Majors later maintained he was sure it was 83. These were the days before the NCAA limited the numbers of scholarships and recruiting visits. Free of restrictions, they scoured Western Pennsylvania's rich countryside, sought speedy skill players in the South, added junior-college transfers. Jackie Sherrill, 29 at the time, virtually lived on the doorstep of the Aliquippa home of Parade all-America running back Tony Dorsett. Majors lured kicker Caron Long from under Penn State's nose by visiting him during a snowstorm, even though he wrecked his car on the way home. The coach worked such long hours, he once fell asleep while touring his new city with a realtor.

On recruiting weekends, the Pitt coach would stand on a podium and hoist an artist's rendering of the planned renovations to Pitt's dark, dank locker room. He talked of carpeting and wooden stalls, plus a weight room where that one outdated machine stood. He promised

promise. "I sold the band without the instruments," Majors said. "But I had the instruments when they showed up."

Could the players carry a tune? He had, after all, inherited a Pitt team that lost 14 of 15 previous games by an average — an average — of 20 points. About a half-dozen returnees walked out of his meet-the-team session. More headed for the exits during the grueling winter conditioning.

"He didn't know very many people, and he didn't care," quarterback Billy Daniels, a junior then, recalled later. "They just killed us. You would do crab crawls. You would do forward crawls. You would roll across the gym floor. Everything imaginable. Guys were flopping like fish all over the place (at Fitzgerald Field House). The other half was behind the bleachers, puking. It was an ugly scene."

If a player messed up, everyone had to do the drill again. "He chased off half the group, and scared the hell out of the rest of us," Daniels added. "But it established that everybody was going to succeed if everybody worked hard; if anybody was lagging, the whole team would be held back."

Johnny Majors was about moving forward, not stepping back. Do the latter in football, and you lose ground, precious yardage.

This gent, remember, was a scorer extraor-

dinaire for his father at Huntland High, amassing a gaudy 565 points. He was a brilliant runner at Tennessee, an all-America who guided the Volunteers to a 10-0 record and No. 2 ranking. He was a studious coach who learned how to win, and brought that knowledge to Iowa State, using speed and a backfield star named George Amundson to make back-to-back bowl trips in 1971 and 1972. That 1971 team lost only to the Nos. 1-2-3 teams that season: Nebraska, Oklahoma and Colorado.

Once at Pitt, he refused to look back — over his history or Pitt's. After all, Jock Sutherland and Pop Warner had coached the Panthers before him and won national titles. Yet Majors bulled forward, like any good running back would. Pitt booster Ed Ifft remembered the coach greeting acquaintances with two questions: Can I win here? Can I recruit here? "When they answered 'yes,' he brought them on board. It was the positive people he wanted to surround himself with."

He refused to allow some shots of Tony Dorsett touchdown runs on his coach's TV program because they showed empty Pitt Stadium seats. He invited to fund-raisers and games actor Lee Majors, who took his hero's name and friendship years before. He pumped up a program, a university, a big city.

"His big hallmark was pride and enthusiasm," Daniels the quarterback added. "He marched to those words. Everything we did was with as much enthusiasm and energy as we could put in it."

There was only once when Majors tried to hide his enthusiasm, his pride. It was the summer of 1973, just before he took Pitt to camp in Johnstown. He was at the Big 33 high school all-star game in Hershey, only a few chairs away from Penn State coach Joe Paterno. The Pitt coach that wondered who would be his tailback come fall — injured Mike Mehalik? Bill Englert? — watched in amazement as his recruit from Hopewell High burned up Big 33 grass: Tony Dorsett. Majors returned to his hotel room, shut the door quietly behind him, then leaped for the ceiling. "Yahoo, we got a tailback."

The next day, Ifft's phone rang. It was Majors. "I'm just calling a few of my friends to tell them we have a running back. But don't tell anybody."

When camp opened with more newcomers (75) than returnees (70), upperclassman tried to pick out the heralded Hopewell back. "There were so many kids, we had a hard time telling who he was," Daniels said. Then, on the first play from scrimmage, Dorsett bolted some 80

After defeating Army in 1976, Majors informs his team of their No. 1 ranking.

yards for a touchdown ... with the excited head coach only a few yards behind.

Camp produced the first controversy of the Majors era. Returnee Lou Cecconi quit the team, claiming Majors and staff mistreated players. Linebacker Kelcy Daviston, a transfer from Arizona State and Frank Kush, seemed to quash any concerns when he offered this: "Heck, this is easy compared to what I've been through."

When the players returned to Oakland's Pitt Stadium, they found their instruments. The locker room was complete. Promise delivered.

There was one other thing found in that new locker room: A message scrawled on the chalkboard by a linebacker. "Jackie Sherrill ain't mean, he's ugly."

Those were fun days, charged by the electricity of the young assistants. Bobby Roper, Joe Madden, Harry Jones, Larry Holton, Bob Matey, Joe Avezzano, Keith Schroeder and Sherrill — all 30 or younger. All plugged into the 38-year-young coach. He was the outlet.

"It was Majors himself, his charisma," Romano said. "Plus, there was his energy."

★   ★   ★

The new coach gave his Panthers new uniforms and helmets, mesh and tearaway jerseys. When they traveled to Georgia for the 1973 opener, amid 80-degree heat, he handed players visors on the sidelines. "That may not seem like a big deal," Daniels said, "but, to us, that was neat stuff." The stuff of winners.

That Sept. 15 afternoon, Majors' underdogs pushed around the tradition-steeped Bulldogs, and between their own Hedges in Sanford Stadium. Dorsett, the reedy freshman, rushed for 101 yards and helped Pitt to score on its first possession of a 7-7 tie.

The team stumbled a bit. It lost the next game, its home opener, when Majors met the post-game media with a cigarette and a soda and spoke of his team's "bonehead football." But that day he dressed 80 players, only 34 of whom had been on the roster for the home finale the year before.

So many freshmen were part of the Majors change: Carson Long, Ashland; Bob Haygood, Atlanta; Tony Dorsett, Aliquippa; Larry Swider, Rockton; John Pelusi, Youngstown, Ohio; Cecil Johnson, Miami, Fla.; Arnie Weatherington, Miami, Fla.; Don Parrish, Tallahassee, Fla.; Ed Wilamowski, Aliquippa. (So many were never seen again, too: Clifton Cransford, Anthony Kozak, Carl Stowe.)

In the season's fifth game, Majors' first foray into West Virginia for the Backyard Brawl, the kids proved all right. Dorsett roared for 110 yards and two touchdowns in the second half, turning a 14-7 halftime advantage into a 25-7 romp. A tone was set. The Panthers were donning sombreros by season's end, recipients of a bid to the third-year Fiesta Bowl. Majors was voted the coach of the year, edging out Okla-

homa rookie Barry Switzer.

Traffic cops and taxi drivers, steel workers and Steel City mothers embraced the small-town boy from Tennessee. "I couldn't buy a meal," the coach said. "Or a beer." He had given the shot-and-a-beer town a shot in the arm.

To be sure, there were potholes.

In 1974, went 7-4 and without a bowl, losing at Notre Dame by 14-10 and at Three Rivers Stadium to Penn State in its first network telecast in a decade. There were some disciplinary problems as well. "I was coming in wondering, 'What will I be looking at today?' "

In 1975, three players were charged with assault and two others charged with theft, all eventually acquitted. On the field, Majors' Panthers were displaying a tenacious 5-2 defense that allowed six opponents one touchdown or none. They were beating Notre Dame by 34-20, thanks to a Notre Dame-record 303 yards from Dorsett, and had three fourth-quarter chances to beat Penn State with a field goal, but failed — admittedly the lowpoint of Majors' Pitt tenure. Majors then lost his top assistant to Washington State as head coach, Sherrill, and won the Sun Bowl over Kansas, 33-19. His play-

Penn State's Joe Paterno and Majors visit at the 1974 Dapper Dan Dinner.

ers carried him off the field after that victory. It wouldn't be the last time.

★ ★ ★

"I had a good feeling in 1976 that we would have a great football team if we didn't have any unusual circumstances." Funny the coach should say that. In the second game, he lost his starting quarterback for the season due to a leg injury, Bob Haygood. In the fifth game, he lost his super backup quarterback, Matt Cavanaugh, to a foot injury. Would you consider starting a walk-on, ex-ninth-stringer an unusual circumstance?

Here was a place and time for that Majors magic, though. The week Tom Yewcic would arise from the ashes to lead the country's second-ranked team, the coach called him into the office. He told the senior he would start that Saturday against Miami. He told him, by the way, he had that scholarship now. "I thought it would be better going into the game with a scholarship quarterback," Majors said later, smiling that wide smile. Top-ranked Michigan lost the day of Yewcic's last start, against Army. Pitt ascended to the top of the polls for the first time since 1937.

The seniors, 37 still on the roster from that 75-strong beginning, wanted to play in the Orange Bowl and soak up the Florida sunshine. Majors wanted to play the next-highest ranked team, which figured to come in the Sugar Bowl.

You can guess who won. The coach sold them again on something.

About this time, embattled Bill Battle was shown the door at Tennessee, and Johnny Majors' alma mater called. He calmly deflected the Pittsburgh questioning and directed the Panthers past Penn State, employing an unbalanced line and Dorsett at fullback for his hometown collegiate finale, a 24-7 victory over their archrival.

Majors took Pitt first to Biloxi, Miss. The better to prepare there for their Sugar Bowl date with destiny. OK, so he pulled the reins off the players, some of whom stayed out until 4 a.m. When the team moved camp to New Orleans, the Big Easy, he gave them a 2 a.m. curfew. At the time, Majors remarked, "Three or four years ago, I had to lock the doors and few times and throw away the keys. But not this time, not with these young men." After all, they had survived Juarez, Mexico, the bowl game before. Bourbon Street was no big deal.

Come New Year's morning, the Panthers gave their coach a proper sendoff, routing the very Georgia team against whom these four magical years all began. Majors was borne aloft in the Superdome after this 27-3 triumph. Pitt was it.

Alas, he was leaving it.

The power of almatism, what Bear Bryant described as "Mama calling," lured Majors back to the land of his football family. Just before the Sugar Bowl, he announced that Johnny would come marching home to Tennessee. He was exit-

ing the big city that he came to embrace.

"The most difficult move I ever made in my life," he said later, after returning to Pitt some 20 years after he first arrived from Iowa State.

"There was no fun in making it. I certainly can't say it was the smartest move. I knew I didn't want to leave Pittsburgh, and the timing was terrible. But I took the challenge. I felt like I had to do it, and I did it. I don't want to sound like a TV preacher.

"I don't think there was ever a more out-standing national championship team. We had all the ingredients. A dominating defense. A great offense with Dorsett and Cavanaugh. A four-year punter in Larry Swider and a four-year kicker in Carson Long. Outstanding per-formers. We were a completely outstanding team.

"Everytime after that, when I came through the (Fort Pitt) tunnel to recruit or play golf with buddies, that hurt. I didn't want to leave here at all.

"We had a great program. We were winning. We worked out a lot of the problems; we fought through a lot of the problems. There was a no more exciting time in my life than the four years I was here."

Yep, Pittsburgh was the place for him.

Majors accepts the Sugar Bowl trophy after Pitt's 27-3 win over Georgia.

No.	Name	Pos.	Class	Ht.	Wt.	Hometown / High School
25	Wayne Adams	QB	SO	6-5	210	Elizabeth/ Elizabeth Forward
8	Joel Anderson	DB	SR	6-0	182	Skokie, IL / Niles West
40	Gary Arcuri	HB	SR	6-1	176	Dallas/ Dallas
26	Mike Balzer	DB	SO	6-1	180	Dunkirk, NY / Dunkirk
88	Allan Barboza	DE/TE	FR	6-2	193	Milestone, KY/ Fleming-Neon
86	Ron Boone	DE	FR	6-5	232	Washington, DC / Eastern
61	Art Bortnick	OG	JR	6-2	248	Euclid, OH / Euclid
71	Kurt Brechbill	OT	FR	6-2	242	Upper St. Clair/ Upper St. Clair
49	Ed Brosky	FB	SR	5-11	207	Carnegie / Chartiers Valley
72	Walt Brown	DT	SO	6-4	243	Allison Park / Shaler
67	Tom Brzoza	OG	JR	6-3	234	New Castle / Neshannock
89	David Bucklew	DE	FR	6-3	214	Pittsburgh / Baldwin
69	Jim Bouy	OG	JR	6-0	237	Miami, FL / Miami Jackson
77	Matt Carroll	OG	SO	6-3	265	Norwood / Interboro
12	Matt Cavanaugh	QB	JR	6-2	209	Youngstown, OH / Cheyney
55	Al Chelsey	LB	SO	6-3	208	Washington, DC / Eastern
62	Steve Clemons	LB	SO	6-3	225	Walnutport / Northhampton
20	Willie Collier	HB/DB	FR	5-10	185	Cordle, GA / Crisp County
84	Rich Cooper	TE	FR	6-4	221	Baltimore, MD / Patapsco
81	Jim Corbett	TE	SR	6-4	210	Erie/ McDowell
58	Jimbo Cramer	LB	SR	6-2	218	Jefferson Boro / Thomas Jefferson
14	Jeff Delancy	MON	SO	6-1	187	Upper St. Clair /Upper St. Clair
35	Dave DeCiccio	MON	SO	6-0	197	Midland / Lincoln
33	Tony Dorsett	HB	SR	5-11	192	Aliquippa / Hopewell
37	Leroy Felder	DB	JR	5-10	191	Baltimore, MD / Northwestern
28	Larry Felton	DB	SR	6-4	202	Cordele, GA / Crisp County
82	Steve Gaustad	TE	SO	6-4	210	New Cumberland / Cedar Cliff
96	Bob Gruber	DE	FR	6-5	232	Greenville / Greenville
64	John Hanhauser	OT	SR	6-2	252	Erie / Cathedral Prep
22	Steve Harris	HB	FR	6-1	185	Williamsport / Williamsport
36	JoJo Heath	HB	FR	5-10	160	Monessen / Monessen
32	Bob Hightower	HB	FR	6-1	190	Buffalo, NY / Baker Victory
63	Jim Hissom	LB	SR	6-2	215	Weirton, WV / Weir
70	Randy Holloway	DT	JR	6-6	240	Sharon / Sharon
34	Robert Hutton	FB	SR	5-11	180	Mahwah, NJ / Mahwah
11	Woody Jackson	QB	FR	6-0	175	Spotslvania, VA / Spotslvania
38	Fred Jacobs	HB	FR	5-9	170	Cincinnati, OH / Wyoming

No.	Name	Pos.	Class	Ht.	Wt.	Hometown / High School
60	Cecil Johnson	DE	SR	6-2	220	Miami, FL / Miami Jackson
24	Gordon Jones	SE	SO	6-1	190	North Vesailles / E. Allegheny
31	Bon Jury	DB	JR	6-0	180	Library / South Park
90`	Kurt Kovach	DE	SR	5-10	210	Southgate, MI / Aquinas
92	Tom Kornick	K	FR	5-10	190	Pittsburgh / Central Catholic
52	Mike Lenosky	LB	SO	6-2	201	Cheswick / Springdale
66	George Link	OG	JR	6-1	247	Uniontown / Laurel Highlands
53	Mike Linn	LB/OG	FR	6-0	224	Steubenville / Steubenville
78	David Logan	MG	SO	6-2	240	Pittsburgh / Peabody
5	Carson Long	K	SR	5-11	203	Ashland / N. Schuylkill
87	Tim Madison	DE	FR	6-3	210	Pittsburgh / Penn Hills
39	Willie Marsh	DB	JR	6-0	180	Newark, NJ / Malcolm Shabazz
16	Scott McKeel	HB/DB	FR	5-10	161	Monaca / Monaca
42	Ron Medley	SE	SR	6-2	192	Madison, VA / Madison, County
76	George Messich	OT	SR	6-4	242	Greensboro/Mapletown/Potomac J.C.
7	Glen Meyer	MON	FR	5-8	180	Glenshaw / Shaler
15	Geroge O'Korn	MON	JR	5-10	200	Lawrence / Canon-McMillan
17	Mark O'Toole	DB	JR	5-11	182	Monroeville / Gateway
68	Don Parrish	DT	SR	6-3	248	Tallahassee, FL / Amos P. Godby
51	Jeff Pelusi	LB	FR	6-0	220	Youngstown, OH / Cheyney
50	John Pelusi	C	SR	6-3	230	Youngstown, OH / Cheyney
94	Steve Pritchard	DT	SO	6-3	240	Washington, DC / Eastern
19	Randy Reutershan	FL	JR	5-11	180	Mahwah, NJ / Mahwah
54	Desmond Robinson	DE	SO	6-0	190	Atlanta, GA / West Fulton
91	Al Romano	MG	SR	6-3	225	Solvay, NY / Solvay/ Stauton Prep
23	Larry Sims	HB	FR	5-10	170	Atlanta, GA / West Fulton
46	Thom Sindewald	FB	SR	6-2	221	Chicago, IL / H.J. Richards
73	Joe Stone	OT	SR	6-4	263	Vandergift / Kiski Area
41	Larry Swider	P	SR	6-3	190	Rockton / DuBois Area
56	John Takacs	C	JR	6-1	230	Youngstown, Ursuline
29	Willie Taylor	FL	JR	6-1	185	Verona, NJ / Verona
34	Elliot Walker	FB	JR	5-11	200	Miami, FL / Miami Jackson
30	Leverga Walker	HB	JR	5-11	180	Miami, FL / Miami Jackson
59	Arnie Weatherington	LB	SR	6-0	195	Miami, FL / Miami Jackson
80	Ed Wilamowski	DE	SR	6-3	211	Aliquippa / Hopewell
27	Carlton Williams	DB	SR	5-8	169	Pahokee, FL / Pahokee
21	J.C. Wilson	DB	JR	6-0	172	Cleveland, OH / Cleveland East
13	Tom Yewcic	QB	SR	5-11	181	Conemaugh / Conemaugh Valley
79	Dan Zelahy	DT	SO	6-3	230	Plum Boro / Plum